Star Light, Star Bright

TEACHER'S EDITION
LEVEL 1

ODYSSEY An HBJ Literature Program

Sam Leaton Sebesta, General Consultant

 Harcourt Brace Jovanovich, Publishers

Orlando   New York   Chicago   Atlanta   Dallas

ISBN 0−15−333360−X

We do not include a Teacher's Edition automatically with each shipment of a classroom set of textbooks. We prefer to send a Teacher's Edition only when requested by the teacher or administrator concerned or by one of our representatives. A Teacher's Edition can be easily mislaid when it arrives as part of a shipment delivered to a school stockroom, and, since it contains answer materials, we want to be sure it is sent *directly* to the person who will use it or to someone concerned with the use or selection of textbooks.

If your classroom assignment changes and you no longer are using or examining this Teacher's Edition, you may wish to pass it on to a teacher who will be using it.

Acknowledgments

The publisher gratefully acknowledges the contribution of Elsa Konig Heald to the preparation of the Teacher's Edition lessons.

For permission to reprint copyrighted material, grateful acknowledgment is made to the following sources:

The Bodley Head: From "Echo and Narcissus" in *Tales the Muses Told* by Roger Lancelyn Green. Copyright © 1965 by Roger Lancelyn Green.

The Dial Press: "I never asked for no allergy" excerpted from the book *Philip Hall Likes Me. I Reckon Maybe* by Bette Greene. Copyright © 1974 by Bette Greene.

E. P. Dutton: From "Bando" (retitled) from *My Side of the Mountain* by Jean George. Copyright © 1959 by Jean George.

Farrar, Straus and Giroux, Inc.: From "The Megrimum" (retitled) from *Kneeknock Rise* by Natalie Babbitt. Copyright © 1970 by Natalie Babbitt.

Four Winds Press, a division of Scholastic Inc.: Four riddles from *The Nonsense Book* by Duncan Emrich. Text copyright © 1970 by Duncan Emrich.

Harcourt Brace Jovanovich, Inc.: From "The Big Wind of '34" abridged from *Grandpa's Farm,* © 1965 by James Flora.

Harper & Row, Publishers, Inc.: Specified excerpt from p. 27 in *The Odyssey of Homer,* translated by Richmond Lattimore. Copyright © 1965, 1967 by Richmond Lattimore. Specified excerpt from *A Tree Grows in Brooklyn* by Betty Smith. Copyright, 1943, by Betty Smith.

Macmillan Publishing Co., Inc.: "The Falling Star" from *Collected Poems* by Sara Teasdale. Copyright 1930 by Sara Teasdale Filsinger, renewed 1958 by Guaranty Trust Co. of New York, Executor. "Mix a Pancake" from *Sing-Song* by Christina G. Rossetti. Macmillan Publishing Co., Inc., 1924.

David McKay Co., Inc. and Mrs. Helen Thurber: From *Plays and How to Put Them On* by Moyne Rice Smith, © 1961 by Moyne Rice Smith. Published by Henry Z. Walck, Inc. Based on the book *The Great Quillow* by James Thurber, published by Harcourt Brace Jovanovich, Inc. Copyright © 1944 by James Thurber. Copyright © 1972 by Helen W. Thurber.

Eve Merriam: Excerpt from "Thumbprint" from *It Doesn't Always Have to Rhyme* by Eve Merriam. Copyright © 1964 by Eve Merriam.

Robert Lescher Literary Agency, Inc.: Quotes by Isaac Bashevis Singer.

Russell & Volkening, Inc. as agent for the author: From "A Wagon Load of Bricks" in *Harriet Tubman: Conductor on the Underground Railroad* by Ann Petry. Copyright © 1955 by Ann Petry.

Scholastic Magazines, Inc.: From *The Crane Maiden* by Miyoko Matsutani. Text copyright © 1968 by Parents' Magazine Press.

Frederick Warne & Company, Inc.: From "The Jumblies" by Edward Lear.

Contents

General Consultant

Sam Leaton Sebesta is on the faculty of the University of Washington in Seattle, where he teaches reading and children's literature. A former elementary grade teacher, Dr. Sebesta has written numerous books and articles in the field of reading, and has earned national recognition for his speeches and workshops on teaching literature. From 1975 to 1979 he was a regional coordinator for Classroom Choices, a joint project of the Children's Book Council and the International Reading Association. Dr. Sebesta received his doctorate from Stanford University.

Consultants

Elaine M. Aoki is an administrator and reading specialist for the Seattle, Washington, public schools and was formerly an elementary school teacher in Auburn, Washington. She received her doctorate in reading from the University of Washington.

Willard E. Bill is an assistant professor and Director of the Indian Teacher Education Program at the University of Washington.

Sylvia Engdahl is an anthologist and author of science fiction and nonfiction for young people. She has written numerous articles on children's literature and is best known for her novel *Enchantress from the Stars,* a Newbery Honor Book.

Carolyn Horovitz is a former librarian in the Santa Monica, California, public schools and the University Elementary School at UCLA. She is the editor of the *Anthology of Children's Literature* (5th ed.) and a past member of the Newbery and Caldecott awards committees.

Daphne P. Muse is a lecturer in children's literature at Mills College in Oakland, California, and a children's book reviewer for KGO-TV (ABC).

Margaret D. Simpson is a specialist in children's books and Director of the Story Theatre Program for the Albany, California, public schools.

Consulting Educators

Sonya Blackman is an assistant manager of the Books Unlimited Cooperative and an instructor in children's literature at the University of California Extension in Berkeley. She received her master's degree in early childhood education from Sonoma State University.

Myra Cohn Livingston is an author and award-winning poet. She is Poet-in-Residence and a teacher of creative writing for the Beverly Hills Unified School District and is a Senior Instructor at the UCLA Extension.

Barre Toelken is a professor of English and Director of the Ethnic Studies Program at the University of Oregon, Eugene, Oregon. Dr. Toelken is a past president of the American Folklore Society and a former editor of the *Journal of American Folklore*.

William Anderson
Department of English
California State University
at Northridge
Northridge, California

Gwen Batey
Teacher
William F. Turnbull Middle
School
San Mateo, California

Dorothy W. Blake
Coordinator of Planning for
Media Resources and
Utilization
Division of Instructional
Planning and Development
Atlanta Public Schools
Atlanta, Georgia

Carlota Cardenas de Dwyer
Department of English
The University of Texas
at Austin
Austin, Texas

John M. Chavez
Educational Consultant
The Urban Institute for Human
Services, Inc.
San Francisco, California

Joan Cheifetz
Principal
Thornhill School
Oakland Unified School District
Oakland, California

Ann Cheleen
Teacher
H. O. Sonnesyn Elementary
School
New Hope, Minnesota

Harold Fenderson
Principal
R. V. Daniels Elementary
School
Jacksonville, Florida

Barbara Friedberg
Teacher
Martin Luther King, Jr.,
Laboratory School
Evanston, Illinois

M. Jean Greenlaw
College of Education
North Texas State University
Denton, Texas

Elsa Konig Heald
Teacher
Sun Valley Elementary School
San Rafael, California

Franklin Koontz
Teacher
Bellevue School District
Bellevue, Washington

Joanne Lincoln
Librarian, Professional Library
Atlanta Public Schools
Atlanta, Georgia

Frances Mackie
Teacher
Detroit Public Schools
Detroit, Michigan

Richard McBreen
Teacher
William F. Turnbull Middle
School
San Mateo, California

Nancy Lofton Morrow
Teacher, retired
Carmel Valley, California

Evelyn Myton-Plantillas
Resource Specialist
San Jose Unified School
District
San Jose, California

E. Renee Nathan
Director of Curriculum and
Special Projects, K-12
Lodi Unified School District
Lodi, California

Ben Nelms
Department of English and
College of Education
University of Missouri
Columbia, Missouri

Elizabeth Nelms
Teacher
Hickman High School
Columbia, Missouri

Soledad P. Newman
Department of English
Miami University
Oxford, Ohio

Kay Palmer
Teacher
Shoreline School District
Shoreline, Washington

Barbara K. Rand
Teacher
Springfield Middle School
Springfield, Pennsylvania

Beverly Remer
Teacher
New York City Public Schools
District 10
New York, New York

Doris Shriber
Teacher
William F. Turnbull Middle
School
San Mateo, California

Barbara M. Shulgold
Teacher
Vallemar Structured School
Pacifica, California

Clarice Stafford
Assistant Superintendent for
Curriculum
Wayne-Westland Schools
Wayne, Michigan

Barbara Tapolow
Teacher
P.S. 124
New York, New York

Ann Terry
School of Professional
Education
University of Houston at Clear
Lake City
Houston, Texas

Kelley Tucker
Teacher
Sun Valley Elementary School
San Rafael, California

Lois Wendt
Teacher
Crystal Heights School
Crystal, Minnesota

ODYSSEY

An HBJ Literature Program, Levels 1-8

odyssey (äd′ ə sē) *n.* A long wandering journey. Your students travel to new places, meet new characters, and discover new insights that deepen their sense of themselves and expand their view of the world…in a word, ODYSSEY. It's an adventure in memorable experiences, an introduction to the riches of the imagination.

In every level, ODYSSEY presents an exceptional variety of quality literature, written by an outstanding selection of classic and contemporary writers.

From Level 1 to Level 8, ODYSSEY will help you inspire your students to read and enjoy literature. ODYSSEY also offers students a solid foundation in literary appreciation and helps build skills in reading, writing, speaking, and listening.

Features of ODYSSEY

• High-interest poems, plays, short stories, science fiction, folk tales, excerpts from biographies and novels, essays, and more.

• Writers who represent the diversity of our society, including E.B. White, Beverly Cleary, Ernesto Galarza, Jamake Highwater, Virginia Hamilton, Laurence Yep, Nicholasa Mohr.

• Dazzling art that enhances each selection.

• A range of reading levels that will appeal to students of various reading abilities.

• A thematic structure that focuses on relationships, adventure, humor, fantasy, and more.

• Skill-building material students can use on their own.

• Student-centered activities that develop literary understanding and appreciation.

Turn the page to see samples of the features you'll find in ODYSSEY.

Here are some examples of the

From Level 1 Primer

Mix a Pancake

A poem by Christina Rossetti

Mix a pancake,
Stir a pancake,
   Pop it in the pan;
Fry the pancake,
Toss the pancake,—
   Catch it if you can.

Your students will enjoy reading the stories, plays, poems, and songs. In ODYSSEY, every student will find selections of interest and appeal.

In every book, students will read selections by award-winning authors— Maurice Sendak, Lucille Clifton, C.S. Lewis, Arnold Lobel, Karla Kuskin, E.L. Konigsburg, Langston Hughes, Taro Yashima, Natalie Babbitt, Laura Ingalls Wilder.

From Level 3

The Big Wind of '34

A tall tale by James Flora
Pictures by Marie-Louise Gay

If you stay around Grandpa long enough, you will hear all sorts of amazing stories about his farm. Some people might call them tall tales, but you can decide for yourself after reading this tale as Grandpa tells it.

When Grandma and I first came to the farm, there was no barn—just a house. We were very poor and couldn't afford to build a barn. We had a cow, and she had to sleep outside. She didn't like that at all. On cold days she would get so angry that she wouldn't give us any milk.

265

Pages reduced. Actual size 7½″ x 9″.

variety you'll find in ODYSSEY

Throughout ODYSSEY, your students will discover authors and illustrators whose ideas and imagery invite their readers back for more.

From Level 5

The Great Quillow

A play by Moyne Rice Smith
based on the story by James Thurber
Illustrated by Sal Murdocca

Characters

Lamplighter	Baker
Town Crier	Candlemaker
Town Clerk	Cobbler
Blacksmith	Carpenter
Tailor	Locksmith
Butcher	Quillow, the Toymaker
Candymaker	Hunder, the Giant

Setting: Village square.
Time: Many years ago.

The village clock strikes seven. Lamplighter enters with his long staff and lights the street lamp.

Hunder sits above our village and curses it. What can we do? He has plundered the villages of the far countryside. And today the earth shook when he strode onto our hillside. He

A Wagon Load of Bricks

A chapter from the biography *Harriet Tubman: Conductor on the Underground Railroad* by Ann Petry
Illustrated by Kenneth Longtemps

From Level 8

Harriet Tubman was a great leader in the fight against slavery in America. Born a slave in Maryland, she ran away and made the dangerous journey North in 1849, when she was twenty-nine. She returned South to conduct other slaves to freedom along the Underground Railroad. Her courage has inspired many writers, like Ann Petry who wrote the biography from which this excerpt is taken. Another such writer is Hildegarde Hoyt Swift, who wrote the following verse as part of a longer poem entitled "I brought to the New World the gift of devotion."

I was Harriet Tubman, who would not stay in bondage.
I followed the devious, uncharted trails to the North,
I followed the light of the North Star,
 I ran away to freedom in 1849.
I was Harriet Tubman who could not stay in freedom,
 While her brothers were enslaved.
. . . .
 I was Harriet Tubman,
 Who "never run my train off the track,
 And never lost a passenger."

FROM 1851 TO 1857, the country moved closer to civil war. During these years Harriet Tubman made eleven trips into Maryland to bring out slaves.

In November, 1856, she rescued Joe Bailey. In the spring she had made two trips to the Eastern Shore.[1] The result of one of these trips is recorded in Still's Underground Railroad:[2] "April 1851

266

T9

Here are more stimulating

Illustrations will help your students visualize story characters, settings, and actions, making literature a more enjoyable experience.

BANDO

From the novel *My Side of the Mountain*
by Jean Craighead George
Illustrated by Lyle Miller

It was late spring when Sam Gribley left his family's crowded New York City apartment home and set out for some land in the Catskill Mountains that his great-grandfather had once tried to farm. He carried only a penknife, a ball of string, an ax, a flint with steel,[1] and forty dollars. He knew how to fish and build fires, and he figured that was all he needed for a new life.

During his first few days in the wilds, Sam was

The Crane Maiden

A Japanese folk tale retold by Miyoko Matsutani
English version by Alvin Tresselt
Illustrated by Masami Miyamoto

Long years ago, at the edge of a small mountain village in the snow country of Japan, there lived an old man and his wife. They had little in this world that they could call their own. But they were happy in their life together.

Now one winter morning the old man set out for the village with a bundle of firewood fastened to his back. It was bitter cold. He knew he would have little trouble selling the wood. Then with the money, he would buy some food so that he and his wife could have a good supper.

As the old man trudged through the falling snow, he was suddenly aware of a fluttering sound, and a pitiful cry of *Koh, koh*. Turning from the path to investigate, he came upon a great crane frantically trying to free herself from a trap.

The old man's heart was touched with pity for the magnificent bird. While he tried to soothe the crane with tender words, his hands released the cruel spring of the trap. At once the crane flew up, joyfully calling *Koh, koh*, and disappeared into the snowy sky.

T10

selections from ODYSSEY

In Levels 1 and 2, wordless picture stories develop visual literacy. By reading and retelling picture stories, students increase their oral vocabulary and their ability to find meaning and "a sense of story" in pictures.

Your students will find units on fantasy, humor, and the natural world throughout the books. In Levels 5 and 8, special units focus on the people, heroes, and events in America's past. Level 7 includes a unit on myths and epics. These thematic units will help you enrich the various curriculum areas you teach.

From Level 1 Preprimer

Pages reduced. Actual size 7½" x 9"

From Level 7

ECHO & NARCISSUS

A GREEK MYTH RETOLD BY ROGER LANCELYN GREEN
ILLUSTRATED BY KATIE THAMER

The gods took a devilish delight in punishment. When someone angered one of them—and the gods were quick to take offense—the offender was tortured in a way that cleverly fit the crime. The goddess Hera, who was forever tracking down her flirtatious husband, Zeus, became particularly skilled at punishing his sweethearts. She changed one beautiful maid into a hairy bear. When Zeus tried to disguise another girl friend as a cow, Hera had a gadfly pursue the cow around the earth. Now the beautiful nymph Echo is about to feel Hera's wrath.

U P ON THE WILD, lonely mountains of Greece lived the Oreades,[1] the nymphs or fairies of the hills, and among them one of the most beautiful was called Echo. She was one of the most talkative, too, and once she talked too much and angered Hera, wife of Zeus, king of the gods.

When Zeus grew tired of the golden halls of Mount Olympus, the home of the immortal gods, he would come down to earth and wander with the nymphs on the mountains. Hera, however, was jealous and often came to see what he was doing. It seemed strange at first that she always met Echo, and that Echo kept her listening for hours on end to her stories and her gossip.

But at last Hera realized that Echo was doing this on purpose to detain her while Zeus went quietly back to Olympus as if he had never really been away.

"So nothing can stop you talking?" exclaimed Hera. "Well, Echo, I do not intend to spoil your pleasure. But from this

1. Oreades (OHR • ee • AHD • eez).

T11

Special features develop literary

Learn About Literature features help students develop an appreciation for literature and an understanding of various literary elements and devices. Students learn about such literary elements as setting, plot, and characterization. They learn to use such literary devices as rhythm, repetition, and figurative language. They become aware of illustration styles, uses of the library, and more.

Literary excerpts and examples are used to help students learn about specific aspects of literature. And activities provide opportunities for students to practice what they are learning.

Learn About
Libraries

Animals in the Library

These books are all mixed up. Some are storybooks. Some are fact books. Can you help me get the books on the right shelves?

I'll find the storybooks.

I'll find the fact books

From Level 5

Learn About
Stories

Characters to Remember

Think about some favorite characters in stories you have read. Were they brave? determined? clever? honest? wicked? These are all *traits*. A character's traits are what make that character stand out in your mind. They are what make a character someone you are likely to remember.

A character's traits may be learned from what that character says. What traits do you detect in Beth from what she says in the following section from the story "I Never Asked for No Allergy"? In this scene, Beth is saying good-bye to her dog, Friendly, because she is allergic to him.

At the kennel I held Friendly close to me while Pa explained about the allergy to Mr. Grant. "You are welcome to swap," he said, reaching out for Friendly.

"Wait!" I said. "A person has got to say good-bye, don't they?" I looked into Friendly's eyes and wondered how I could make him

understand. "I never wanted to get rid of you, Friendly. I only wanted to get rid of the aller—*Her-her-choo!*—of the allergy."

Caring, sensitive, concerned— these are traits you may have observed in Beth from what she says.

A character's traits also may be learned from what the author tells us. Here is the way author Natalie Babbitt describes Egan as he begins to climb the mountain in the story "The Megrimum."

. . . Egan was half an hour ahead by that time. And he was young and strong, alone—and determined.

Later in that story, the traits of being *strong* and *determined* are shown in what Egan does—in his actions.

Egan, deep in the mist, heard nothing. He wandered up the final stony slope toward the top like a sleepwalker lost in dreams. . . . And then he stopped, chilled suddenly out of his trance. Just ahead there came a noise as of an animal thrashing about, and the low rumble of a voice.

He crept forward, grasping the nearly forgotten stick tightly,

and his heart pounded. The Megrimum! At last, the Megrimum! Slay it, perhaps—perhaps; but at least he would see it.

More thrashing in the weeds ahead. "Owanna-ooowanna," the voice seemed to murmur.

Closer and closer crept Egan and then he saw it dimly, all flailing arms, rolling about on the ground.

209

T12

understanding and appreciation

Choose a book for each animal.

I like dinosaurs. Where can I find out more about them?

I have a new pet ant. What can I feed her?

1

M
hear a
I read

3

At the primary levels, *Learn About Literature* features focus on such literary elements and devices as story characters, story sequence, sound words, story structure, plots, poetry, and more.

At the intermediate levels, there are features about plays, writing quatrains (four-line poems) and limericks, figurative language, biography, characterization, and theme.

In Levels 7 and 8, these features cover a variety of topics, including writing a newspaper, performing Readers Theatre, learning about science fiction and fantasy, writing humorous essays, understanding poetry, and learning how authors use setting and point of view. There are several *Learn About Literature* features in each book at Levels 1-6, five in Level 7, and six in Level 8.

Learn About

On Stage!   **Plays**

The theater lights dim. The curtain goes up. You are about to see a play. As the actors move and speak, you find out what is happening. With the costumes and scenery, you picture the time and place.

A play is meant to be performed. That is the main difference between a play and a story. When it is written, a play *looks* different, too. It has

a cast of characters

Characters	Mrs. Brown	Paddington
	Mrs. Bird	Nurse

stage directions

(Paddington *comes in carrying a letter.*)

dialogue

Paddington: There's a letter for you, Mrs. Brown. It looks like Mr. Curry's writing.

Mrs. Brown: Yes, I'm afraid you're right.

How does a story look different from a play?

1 Does it have characters?

2 Does it have stage directions?

3 Does it have dialogue?

You will find this bear's answers below.

3 A story does have dialogue, but the dialogue is usually in quotation marks.

2 A story does not have stage directions, but it does tell what the characters do and how they feel. This information is not in parentheses.

1 A story does have characters, but they are not listed at the b... in a cast of characters

T13

282

ODYSSEY includes skill-building material students can do on their own

Questions and Activity pages foster students' critical reading and creative writing skills. You'll find this feature at the end of most prose selections to help you enhance the reading and writing skills you teach.

By including levels of questions that range from simple (recall and inference) to more complex (extrapolation and relating reading to experience), students may test their literal, interpretive, and critical reading skills. Activities provide opportunities for a range of responses, from speaking and writing, to drawing and performing.

In levels 7 and 8, special *Understanding Literature* sections along with the *Questions* and *Activities* add to students' knowledge and appreciation of various literary elements and techniques. The questions, activities, and composition assignments at these levels help students learn skills of self-expression, how to identify the theme of a story, explore the use of repetition for effect, create a story sequence, and more.

Questions

Who am I?

1. I gobble up goats.
2. I get fat.
3. I go "trip, trap, trip, trap."
4. I am not in this story.

bridge

Gunniwolf

goat

Troll

Activity

Here come three fat Billy Goats Gruff.
The ugly Troll has gone away.
Who waits under the bridge now?
Draw it.
Name it.
What will it say?

Questions

1. Billy made two state... might be fibbing. Wh...

2. When did Encyclope... had a *problem?*

3. What did Encyclope... to try to *solve* the p...

4. Why did the author... story, not within it?

5. In this story, a susp...
   a. is the wrongdoer...
   b. might be the wrongdoer.
   c. is innocent, but is accused of being the wrongdoer.

Activity

If Encyclopedia Brown had not found Sally's roller skates, he might have put an advertisement in a newspaper, offering a reward for their return. Write an advertisement for Encyclopedia. In your advertisement, tell what the skates looked like, and where and when they were last seen.

T14

21

These special features will help your students appreciate literature even more

About the Author features give readers a glimpse into the lives of authors. Quotes that provide insights into the authors' ideas and techniques, and information on how authors began their careers, help students to see authors as real people.

From Level 6

About ISAAC BASHEVIS SINGER

Isaac Bashevis Singer's stories are set in Jewish communities much like those he knew as a young boy growing up in Poland in the early 1900s. His father was a rabbi (a leader or teacher of the Jewish religion), and his mother was a rabbi's daughter. Although he studied to become a rabbi, Isaac Bashevis Singer found work as a journalist instead. In 1935 he came to the United States and got a job on New York's *Jewish Daily Forward,* a newspaper written in Yiddish, a language spoken by many Jewish people of European background. Mr. Singer says, ''When I came here, I said to my editor, 'What I want is a steady job.' He replied, 'A steady job? In a language that will die in ten years?' Yet, you see, Yiddish is still with us.''

Isaac Bashevis Singer continues to write his stories in Yiddish, and then supervises their translation into English. His stories, however, have been praised for their appeal to people of all cultures. In 1979 he was given the Nobel Prize for Literature, the highest honor a writer can receive.

More Books by Isaac Bashevis Singer

Zlateh the Goat and Other Stories
The Fearsome Inn
A Day of Pleasure: Stories of a Boy Growing Up in Warsaw

From Level 4

BOOKSHELF

The Ghost on Saturday Night by Sid Fleischman. Little, Brown, 1974. Opie guides a mean-looking stranger through the thick fog. His reward is two tickets to a ghost-raising. Opie doesn't know he has front-row seats to a bank robbery, too.

The Trouble with Jenny's Ear by Oliver Butterworth. Little, Brown, 1960. When Jenny hears thoughts before they are spoken, she begins to wonder what is wrong with her.

Katie John by Mary Calhoun. Harper & Row, 1960. Katie John thinks she is going to spend a boring summer in Missouri. Then a neighbor tells her that the house Katie is staying in is haunted.

A-Haunting We Will Go; Ghostly Stories and Poems collected by Lee Bennett Hopkins. Albert Whitman, 1977. Some of these ghost stories and poems will make you laugh. Some will make you shiver.

The Shrinking of Treehorn by Florence Parry Heide. Holiday House, 1971. Treehorn sees that shelves are getting higher, and his clothes are getting looser. Can he really be shrinking?

119

At the end of each textbook, Levels 4-8, definitions of important words provide independent vocabulary study.

A list of key literary terms appears at the end of each textbook, Levels 6-8. Definitions as well as examples taken from the selections help to explain the meaning and use of each literary element or device.

To encourage independent reading, *Bookshelf* provides an annotated list of books that students may read on their own for enjoyment and for further study of each unit theme. This feature appears at the end of each unit in Levels 2-8.

Annotated Teacher's Editions

Teacher's Editions provide you with all the material you need to teach each lesson: objectives, pre-reading information and suggestions, post-reading discussion questions and enrichment activities. Lessons are annotated directly on the student's pages appearing in each Teacher's Edition.

From Level 2 Teacher's Edition

Most selections have at least two objectives. Some objectives focus on literary appreciation and an understanding of literature and literary elements. Other objectives show how literature relates to human experience.

Synopses provide summaries of the main points of the story or play.

The reading level of each prose selection is designated as "easy," "average," or "challenging."

Objectives ● To enjoy the humor of a play based on trickery and misunderstandings among the characters. ● To identify character traits by extending a story. ● To perform a play using Story Theater techniques.

Synopsis of the Play A donkey, a dog, a cat, and a rooster travel to Bremen to become musicians. During their journey they discover three robbers feasting inside a house. The hungry animals give a screeching musical concert to frighten the robbers away from their meal. Later that night one of the robbers enters the house, only to be ambushed by the animals. Thinking that goblins are haunting the house, the robbers run away for good.

The Traveling Musicians

Reading Level Challenging

218

Pages reduced. Actual size 7½" x 9".

Where appropriate, a background section provides such useful information as historical or geographical details, cultural or ethnic background, and awards won by the book or author.

Introductory material often sets the mood of each selection or relates the subject or theme to something familiar to students, establishing a purpose for reading each selection.

Key vocabulary words needed for students to understand the selection are listed. Page numbers identify the location where each word first appears.

Introducing the Play *As long as there have been people, there have been folk tales. Folk tales were not written down at first, but were told and retold as stories throughout the years. During the 1800s, Jacob and Wilhelm Grimm collected many of the German folk tales that they had heard. One of these is* The Traveling Musicians, *a story about four friends who want to be musicians.*

Word to Know
    musicians (myŏŏ·zish′·ənz): performers or composers of music. (Point to the word in the title.)

Characters

Storyteller 1	**Dog**	**Robber 1**
Storyteller 2	**Rooster**	**Robber 2**
Donkey	**Cat**	**Robber 3**

Storyteller 1:   Once there was a donkey who had worked for his master for many years. At last he grew too old to carry wheat to the mill. His master did not want him any more.

Donkey: My body is weak, but my voice is still strong. I think I will go to the town of Bremen and sing for my living.

Pronounced /brem′·ən/. Bremen is a port city in northwestern Germany.

Brief marginal notes provide pronunciations and definitions of words and clarify and highlight portions of the text.

Storyteller 2:   So the donkey ran away. On the way to Bremen he met a dog. She was lying by the side of the road panting.

219

Lesson continued on next page. ▶

Discussion Questions encourage students to interpret and apply what they have read.

Optional group and individual activities encourage a wide range of student response through composition, oral interpretation, dramatization, art, and other forms of expression.

From Level 2 Teacher's Edition

Discussion Question *When the robber returned to the house, each animal did something to frighten him away. How could a goat, a pig, a cow, and a kangaroo have frightened the robber?* (Possible answers: a goat could butt; a pig could grunt; a cow could bite; a kangaroo could box.)

Enriching Activities   1. *Story Theater.* Have the children perform the play using Story Theater techniques. Some children might read the parts of the storytellers and the characters while others pantomime the characters' actions. See the front of this book for Story Theater techniques.   **2.** *Music.* Ask the children to mimic the sounds of different animals. Then have them combine their sounds in an animal chorus.

Questions

1. Who were the four musicians?

2. One robber saw two lights. What were the lights?

3. The robber said he heard a goblin shout, ''Cook him in a stew.'' What was *really* said?

4. What do you think is the funniest part of this play?

1. Literal / recall
The dog; the cat; the donkey; the rooster. (page 219)
2. Interpretive / inference   The cat's eyes. (page 228)
3. Literal / recall
''Cock-a-doodle-doo-o!'' (page 229)
4. Critical / relating to experience   This question is open to personal opinion, so expect different answers from the children.

Answers to the questions in the student's book are given on the same page as the student questions. Page numbers provide references for re-reading.

Each question is identified by two labels (e.g., literal/ recall). The first label refers to the type of reading skill students must use to answer the question. The second label identifies the type of question being asked.

Activity

The four friends in the story lived together and shared the work. Tell what job each one did. Draw a picture or write one sentence about each animal.

Interpretive / extrapolation
Drawing / writing. Encourage the children to recall the natural abilities of each animal, but do not discourage imaginative answers.

231

T18

A special guide for the teacher

"Teaching Literature in the Classroom" is a special guide for the teacher who wants to enrich and extend students' reading of literature. It includes suggestions for such activities as dramatization, writing, language, and art projects.

From Levels 1-8 Teacher's Editions

Teaching Literature in the Classroom   *Sam Leaton Sebesta*

I hear, and I forget.
I see, and I remember.
I do, and I understand.

Chinese proverb

AS TEACHERS, we want children and young people to discover the joy of reading literature. With this discovery, they become free to pursue this pleasure independently, now and throughout their lifetimes. But we want something more for the young people we teach. We want them to be able to read literature not only with pleasure, but also with understanding. We want them to be able to respond thoughtfully to their reading—to *interact* with it—so that both their pleasure and their knowledge are increased.

Students' interaction with literature begins with teachers who approach literature with joy and excitement. Once a teacher shares this enthusiasm with students, the stage is set for their own interaction with literature, which can be as multifaceted as the teacher and the students wish to make it. This interaction can also be fostered by a good literature program that offers teachers both depth and breadth of selection, as well as providing a structure for helping students to understand and appreciate literature.

Good literary instruction proceeds in a two-phase cycle. First, reading a good selection motivates students to respond expressively to what they have read. Second, proper guidance of their responses enables students to build knowledge and skills that help them understand the next selection they encounter. The goal of such a process is students' continued reading and increasing enjoyment of literature.

The following discussion will provide a number of general guidelines as well as practical ideas for using literature in the classroom. The ideas are divided into four sections, beginning with the reading experience and discussion of literature and then considering other responses to literature— oral and written composition, interpretive reading and dramatization, and the arts. Methodological questions are raised and answered as each section and its activities are developed. Many suggestions for activities are also included throughout the lessons in this Teacher's Edition.

The Reading Experience

PREPARING FOR READING

For beginning readers, the first reading of a poem or a story is a shared experience, with the teacher reading aloud and the students joining in on a refrain or a predictable passage. Beyond this stage, students can be expected to read selections independently, but guidance and motivation are still important. The Teacher's Editions for this program offer suggestions for such guided preparation for reading: questions to raise

T30

Introduction to ODYSSEY

Tell me, Muse, of the man of many ways, who was driven
far journeys, after he had sacked Troy's sacred citadel.
Many were they whose cities he saw, whose minds he learned of,
many the pains he suffered in his spirit on the wide sea,
struggling for his own life and the homecoming of his companions.
. . . .
. . . Goddess, daughter of Zeus, speak, and begin our story.

The Odyssey of Homer

THE "MAN OF MANY WAYS" was Odysseus—king of Ithaca in ancient Greece, hero in the war against Troy, husband of Penelope, father of Telemachus, and, in all his endeavors, a man of unusual cunning and courage. Homer's great epic poem the *Odyssey* recounts Odysseus' long wandering journey home from the Trojan War. Three thousand years later, the *Odyssey* remains one of the enduring works of literature, and Odysseus, one of the enduring heroes.

When we hear the word *odyssey* today, we think of more than the epic journey of Odysseus. For as the word has become part of our language, it has taken on other meanings: a long wandering, a series of adventurous journeys marked by many changes of fortune, an intellectual or spiritual quest. In its broadest sense, we could say that odyssey describes the lifelong journey that all people undertake from birth.

It is that continuing human odyssey and our continuing wonder about it that are at the center of all literature. Though it is history that records our deeds, it is literature that seeks to express our thoughts, feelings, dreams, and wonderings about the world.

Since its origins in the chants and tales of unknown storytellers, literature has recorded events vividly, recalled our shared experience, and taught us about ourselves. In doing so, it has come to us in diverse forms—both oral and written—and in divergent voices, the sum of which is our literary heritage, drawn from the past and growing into the future.

Children's literature is one part of our literary heritage that has experienced remarkable growth in this century. With more than forty thousand children's books in print, the range of genres and content available to young people today is far greater than ever before.

While there is no lack of literature for children, however, the problem of selecting reading can be a difficult one. Some literary works meet children's interests better than others do. There are books that may be more suitable for children at a particular developmental stage or that may offer greater aesthetic growth because of their style, content, or theme. Young people need help in selecting literature that offers the best foundation both for their reading pleasure now, and for a lifetime.

In many instances, that foundation is begun at home, when parents read aloud to their children, share books with them, and talk with them about what they have read. In others, it may begin at school, when teachers and librarians read to students, encourage them to read independently, and support their spontaneous responses to reading. To a large extent, basal reading programs build on that foundation by providing a range of literature for learning and enjoyment throughout the grade levels.

In basal reading programs, however, the literature strand is only one strand in many, and the development of such basic reading skills as decoding and comprehension usually takes precedence over skills of literary appreciation and understanding. In addition, literature is often used as a vehicle to teach skills in the language arts or to enrich and extend other content areas. Despite our best efforts to provide students with a "basic education," we have often forgotten that literature is a basic subject that deserves its own place in the elementary school curriculum.

Purposes of ODYSSEY

ODYSSEY is a carefully planned program designed to provide children with a basic literary education. The program's selections and instructional material are all aimed toward its main objective: to provide a solid foundation of literary experiences on which students may build a lifetime of reading pleasure. To reach this objective, ODYSSEY has the following goals:

- To offer students a wide variety of pleasurable, independent reading of the highest literary quality
- To demonstrate the value of literature and to foster interest in reading

- To increase understanding of literature's relationship to human experience
- To develop insights into personal thoughts, feelings, and experiences
- To promote recognition of the individual's role in the community and society
- To develop an awareness of other people and cultures
- To show the power and possibilities of language as a tool for self-expression and to develop an awareness of the persuasive or manipulatory power of words
- To develop an understanding of literary forms, techniques, and styles
- To demonstrate the unique artistry of individual authors and illustrators
- To encourage thoughtful and critical responses to literature and to develop respect for the responses of others
- To develop the skills of reading comprehension, writing, and the other language arts, as well as logical thinking skills

Criteria for Selections

In choosing selections for ODYSSEY, the program's developers consulted children's literature specialists, teachers, librarians—and children and young people themselves. After potential selections were identified, program consultants (see pages T4 and T5) evaluated each selection using the following criteria:

Interest Level. Is the selection likely to interest children at this age level?

Reading Level. Will most of the children at this level be able to read the selection independently?

Quality. Does the selection have high literary quality?

Experience.   Is the selection worthwhile, either because it brings pure enjoyment to young readers or because it fosters their personal growth?

Portrayal of Ethnic, Minority, and Special Groups.   Does the selection portray all groups fairly?

Further considerations were the selections' relevance to six thematic strands and their balance in such areas as content, literary type, multicultural representation, and authorship. The final choices were made after extensive classroom testing.

Organization of ODYSSEY

The literature in ODYSSEY is organized thematically around six strands. Beginning with Reader One, the strands form the basis of six thematic units in each textbook.

STRANDS IN ODYSSEY

GROWING AND CHANGING	Roles, relationships, and personal growth
ADVENTURE AND SUSPENSE	Real and imaginary adventures
HUMOR	The humorous side of life
FANTASY	Realms of the imagination
EARTH, SEA, AND SPACE	Humans and the natural world
QUEST AND HEROISM	The many aspects of courage

The thematic strands in the program appear in the chart on pages T24 and T25.

Readability in ODYSSEY

In ODYSSEY, prose selections below grade level are usually labeled *Easy,* selections at grade level are labeled *Average,* and selections above grade level are labeled *Challenging.* The selections were evaluated on the basis of their syntactic and conceptual difficulty as well as by the appropriate readability formula.

Level One.   Because most first-grade children are not independent readers, the selections in the three textbooks at Level One are intended for teacher-directed reading and for shared reading experiences. For example, the teacher might begin by reading aloud a selection such as a poem with a refrain or a story with repetition or predictable ''next sentences.'' The teacher can then invite the class to ''take the next part'' or to read aloud in unison. Simple plays—usually presented in the Readers Theatre format—provide still more opportunities for shared reading experiences. To promote oral language development, the Level One readers include content-rich pictures and wordless picture stories so that children may tell or write the story they ''read'' in the illustrations. Some easy stories, which are labeled as such in the Teacher's Editions, can be read independently by able readers.

Levels Two through Eight.   At Levels Two and Three, most prose selections meet the reading abilities of average and above-average readers, with the majority of the selections falling within the average range, as determined mainly by the Spache readability formula. At Levels Four through Eight, most selections continue to meet the reading abilities of the average reader, with the range of reading levels widening to include more selections for below-average and gifted readers. Readability of Levels Four through Eight has been determined mainly by the Dale-Chall readability formula. Since the Dale-Chall readability level of much adult literature is seventh- to eighth-grade, however, in Levels Seven and Eight the label *Challenging* means at or above seventh-grade level; *Average,* sixth grade; *Easy,* fifth grade and below.

Evaluation in the Program

In evaluating the program's success in the classroom, the central question should be whether the selections have enhanced the students' enjoyment of literature. This is an affective outcome that no written test can assess, but teachers can assess progress informally, asking students for their opinions about the literature; listening to their spontaneous comments, especially their expressions of interest in reading and literature; and observing whether they seek out further literary experiences. Brief anecdotal records of the students' responses will provide valid and direct evidence that the program's goal is being met.

The questions and activities in the program can be used to evaluate the students' knowledge of literary elements and techniques, and their growth in literary appreciation, reading comprehension, and both oral and written composition. Questions at the literal level will yield brief yet adequate information on students' abilities in literal comprehension. Questions at the interpretive level can provide information about students' abilities to make inferences, to express opinions based on their reading, and to substantiate both kinds of responses. Questions that require critical thinking skills can assess students' abilities to read "beyond the lines," that is, to integrate what they have read with their own experience or to apply it in a different context. Even though their answers to critical-level questions are subjective and thus will vary greatly, the students' responses can be evaluated in terms of their fluency, flexibility, elaboration, originality, and logic.

Literature for a Lifetime

A literature program for children requires faith in the lasting effects of teaching and learning. Such faith seems warranted. Most adults who like to read literature can describe one or a hundred rewarding contacts with books in childhood and adolescence. Many such readers might identify with Francie, the child in Betty Smith's novel *A Tree Grows in Brooklyn,* who realizes suddenly the benefits of having learned to read:

> From that time on, the world was hers for the reading. She would never be lonely again, never miss the lack of intimate friends. Books became her friends and there was one for every mood. There was poetry for quiet companionship. There was adventure when she tired of quiet hours. There would be love stories when she came into adolescence and when she wanted to feel a closeness to someone she could read a biography. On that day when she first knew she could read, she made a vow to read one book a day as long as she lived.

The journeys children take through books can carry them as near as a city street or as far away as a dragon's lair; but wherever their reading leads them, the discovery of literature in childhood can extend and enrich their lives far beyond that time. In books readers may live more lives, try on more costumes, step into more situations than any one life could possibly afford. ODYSSEY is just the beginning of that life-long journey through literature.

Thematic Strands in ODYSSEY

Level	GROWING AND CHANGING	ADVENTURE AND SUSPENSE	HUMOR
1★	*Let's Go Together* Relationships with friends and family	*Far, Far Away* The call of adventure	*What a Surprise!* Humorous experiences with an element of surprise
2	*We Could Be Friends* The many aspects of friendship	*Something Is There* Mysterious happenings	*Tell Me Something Very Silly* Comical characters; improbable occurrences
3	*Good Times* Building relationships	*You Can't Catch Me* Ingenious escapes from danger	*It's Not Funny* Humorous predicaments
4	*When Paths Cross* Contrasting points of view	*Across the Land and Sea* Journeys to new lands	*What a Character!* Remarkable characters in humorous situations
5	*Never Give Up* The role of perseverance in personal growth	*Facing the Unknown* Suspenseful encounters in different settings	*It Must Be a Trick* Tricksters and trickery
6	*Dream Keepers* Recognizing individual identity and talents	*Expect the Unexpected* Unexpected encounters and surprise endings	*Funny Side Up* Mix-ups, mishaps, and misunderstandings
7	*Reflections* Experiences leading to personal growth and life changes	*On a Moonless Night* Strange occurrences	*Monkey Business* The techniques of humor
8	*Spectrum* The many paths to self-knowledge and maturity	*Only Darkness Ticking* The techniques of suspense	*On the Funny Side* Humor in ordinary and extraordinary situations

★Refers only to Level 1 Reader. Strands are not grouped by units in Preprimer and Primer.

FANTASY	EARTH, SEA, AND SPACE	QUEST AND HEROISM
Tell Me a Story Adventures of fantasy characters	*I Wonder* The wonders of nature	*I'm Growing* Awareness of physical growth
Long, Long Ago Magical beings, places, and things	*Animals All Around* Animals and their environments	*I Can Do It!* Acting independently and assuming new roles
Would You Believe It! Tall tales	*There Is a Season . . .* The cycle of the seasons	*Tell Me the Name* Awareness of personal identity
When the Moon Shines Illusions and transformations	*To Live with Animals* Relationships between animals and humans	*Problems and Puzzles* Meeting challenges and solving problems
Truly Amazing Talents Characters with amazing or unusual talents	*To Live with Nature* Living with the creatures and forces of nature; survival	*From America's Past* Characters and events from American history
Time Travelers Exploring time through fantasy	*A Tree of Ice,* *A Rain of Stars* Nature as a source of inspiration and beliefs	*Tests of Courage* The many forms of courage in myth, legend, and contemporary life
A Gift of Story Greek myths and epic heroes	*Voices from the Earth* Encounters with animals and elements in nature	*To Stand Alone* Individual courage in the face of adversity
Another Where, *Another When* The elements and varieties of fantasy	*Secrets* The interrelationship of humans and nature	*We, the People* The importance of ordinary people in American history

Skills Index for Preprimer

This Skills Index will help you to locate the pages on which each listed skill is presented in a level of ODYSSEY: AN HBJ LITERATURE PROGRAM. Boldfaced page references indicate that the skill is presented in the pupil's textbook. Other references are to teaching suggestions and activities in the Teacher's Edition.

The numbers preceding the items in the index correspond to the HBJ Skills Code. This code may be used to correlate skills in ODYSSEY with other language arts and reading programs published after 1980 by Harcourt Brace Jovanovich. Teachers who wish to cross-reference these programs may do so by referring to these same numbers that appear in other programs. The index can also serve as a basis for correlating ODYSSEY with the management system or curriculum guide used in your school.

Skills Code Number	SKILL	PAGES
	READINESS	
1.1	**To Promote Social and Emotional Development**	
1.1.1	to increase self-confidence	**10–13, 22–33**
1.1.4	to express feelings and emotions	36–37, 40–41
1.1.6	to be aware of home environment	**10–13, 20–21**
1.1.9	to be aware of the natural environment	**22–33,** 53
1.3	**To Promote Cognitive Development**	
1.3.1	to recognize, understand, and name space relationships	15, 38, 48–49
1.5	**To Visually Discriminate, to Remember, to Match**	
1.5.6	to identify or name letters	36–37, **38–39**
	COMPREHENSION	
3.1	**To Recognize Concepts**	
3.1.4	to relate reading to experience	8, 10–13, 14, 16, 20–21, 33, 34–35, 40–41, 47, 53, 62, 63, 64
3.2	**To Classify**	
3.2.1	to classify by common attributes or association	51

Activities Index

Teaching Literature in the Classroom

Sam Leaton Sebesta

I hear, and I forget.
I see, and I remember.
I do, and I understand.

Chinese proverb

AS TEACHERS, we want children and young people to discover the joy of reading literature. With this discovery, they become free to pursue this pleasure independently, now and throughout their lifetimes. But we want something more for the young people we teach. We want them to be able to read literature not only with pleasure, but also with understanding. We want them to be able to respond thoughtfully to their reading—to *interact* with it—so that both their pleasure and their knowledge are increased.

Students' interaction with literature begins with teachers who approach literature with joy and excitement. Once a teacher shares this enthusiasm with students, the stage is set for their own interaction with literature, which can be as multifaceted as the teacher and the students wish to make it. This interaction can also be fostered by a good literature program that offers teachers both depth and breadth of selection, as well as providing a structure for learning to understand and appreciate literature.

Good literary instruction proceeds in a two-phase cycle. First, reading a good selection motivates students to respond expressively to what they have read. Second, proper guidance of their responses enables students to build knowledge and skills that help them understand the next selection they encounter. It is a cyclical process that leads students to turn toward literature instead of away from it.

The following discussion will provide a number of general guidelines as well as practical ideas for using literature in the classroom. The ideas are divided into four sections, beginning with the reading experience and discussion of literature and then considering other responses to literature—oral and written composition, interpretive reading and dramatization, and the arts. Methodological questions are raised and answered as each section and its activities are developed. Many suggestions for activities are also included throughout the lessons in this Teacher's Edition.

The Reading Experience

PREPARING FOR READING

For beginning readers, the first reading of a poem or a story is a shared experience, with the teacher reading aloud and the students joining in on a refrain or a predictable passage. Beyond this stage, students can be expected to read selections independently, but guidance and motivation are still important. The Teacher's Editions for this program offer suggestions for such guided preparation for reading: questions to raise before the reading takes place; brief comments about the work that is to be read; and *definitions* of key terms to help students understand the selection.

Preparation need only take a few moments, but it is useful for several reasons. It allows students to begin reading with a "warmed-up motor," prepared to respond to the selection. It helps students establish a focus for reading. And it helps remove the barriers that unfamiliar words may otherwise present. Research has shown that preteaching relevant vocabulary increases student comprehension.

SILENT AND ORAL READING

Most reading specialists recommend that first readings always be silent, independent readings. They point out that silent reading permits each student to read at his or her own pace. It encourages reflection and allows both time for response and the chance to go back and *reread* a passage before going on. Initial silent reading helps students enjoy and interpret a selection further during a later oral reading.

This recommendation for silent reading first has exceptions. Most poems should be read aloud initially. Anecdotes and funny stories beg for sharing and may lose their appeal if assigned to be read silently. When the language or theme of a selection is complex, guided oral reading helps students share the literary experience from the start.

At no time, however, should oral reading be considered a mere exercise in "getting all the words right." Rather, it is a means to guiding understanding. Most often, this guidance is better done by (1) *preparing students to read silently*, (2) *encouraging silent reading according to each student's rate and reading strategies*, and (3) *later having students reread all or part of a selection for a purpose— to support a point, to share an enthusiasm, or to enliven a work through oral interpretation or dramatization.*

DISCUSSING A SELECTION

Once a selection is read, discussion can enhance the literary experience. The main purpose of such discussion is to allow students to speak, to express their responses to the literature they are reading, and to listen to the varied responses of their classmates. In addition, discussion can be an informal way for you to assess students' enjoyment, involvement, and understanding of what they have read. Asking a general opening question and inviting students to ask questions are good ways to begin a discussion that leads to more structured questions and activities.

Opening discussion should be nonthreatening. It should invite immediate, pertinent response. It should, if possible, set the stage for more focused questions and activities. Here are three effective ways to begin a discussion. (Consult each selection in the Teacher's Edition for specific suggestions.)

1. *Ask what students discovered as a result of their reading.* Sometimes this may be a focusing question, based on a preparation question posed before the reading. Sometimes the question can be a more general opener—"Tell me about the story"—that invites students to share their responses, fresh from reading, without imposing a structure.

2. *Refer to the question-and-activity page in the pupil's textbook,* which is included after most of the longer prose selections. Students who have prepared responses to items on the page will have something to contribute at once, and discussion will get off to a good start.

3. *Ask each student to find one passage in the story that is exciting to read aloud*—a segment that might entice a listener to read the entire story. Subsequent discussion can begin with a request for justification: "Why did you choose that part?"

Early in the discussion, invite student questions: "What did you wonder about as you read the story? Did a question come to your mind as you read this poem?" Such a procedure encourages self-generated questioning as one reads, a basic strategy that good readers use constantly.

Inquiry Within the Program.   In ODYSSEY, a variety of questions help teachers focus and extend discussions about literature, and also help provide well-rounded, unified lessons. Some of the questions are derived from objectives stated in the teaching notes preceding each selection. Others review objectives from earlier readings or seek to broaden the lesson. In each case, questions pertain to the central meaning and significance of the work, their chief purpose being to enhance students' enjoyment and understanding and to allow them to use their listening, speaking, and writing skills when responding.

The following are the five types of questions used in the ODYSSEY program:

1. **Recall** *questions ask the student to specify information, or data, present in the story, poem, or nonfiction selection.* Students are not asked to recall random facts, but information derived from the focus of the selection. Often this information is used in subsequent higher-level discussion. With some students, the recall level needs little attention. With others, you may need to elicit additional recall, such as sequence of events, before proceeding to discuss a selection above the literal level.

2. **Inference** *questions are based on the information given in a selection, but they require more than simple recall.* Inference questions require conjectures from the student based on knowledge of the selection's content, on personal experience, and on imagination The author of a story, for example, may present three details, three "facts" about the setting from which the reader is expected to infer additional details. Many readers do this automatically, but some do not. Inference questions, then, give practice and encouragement in figuring out what happened between events described in a story, in determining whose point of view is presented in a poem, or in speculating about cause and effect when the relationship is implied rather than directly described. This question type recognizes that no literary work *tells* all. Rather, every literary work *suggests*, and the reader interacts by inferring the missing parts. Much of the fun of reading literature comes from inference.

3. **Extrapolation** *questions, extensions of inference, invite the reader to consider, for example, what happened* after *the story ended, how a character might act in another situation, or what the speaker of a poem might say about an object or scene other than that described in the poem.* (*To extrapolate* means "to project, extend or expand something that is known into an unknown area; to conjecture.") Extrapolation questions are often more extensive and more speculative than inference questions, and they may extend creative thinking toward writing, drawing, or speaking.[1]

4. **Relating reading to experience** *questions, as the term is used here, are those questions that invite the reader to relate the literary work directly to his or her own life.* The basic form for this question is "How is your own experience *like* something in the selection you have just read?" A variation is "Based on your experience, what would you have done in the situation described in

---

1. Robert A. Collins, "Extrapolation: Going Beyond the Present," *Media and Methods*, 16, no. 3 (November 1979); 22–25.

this selection?'' Throughout the program, this basic idea is varied to meet the specifics of a story, a poem, or a work of nonfiction.

5. **Language and vocabulary** *questions are closed-answer items to check a reader's knowledge of key terms, idioms, or stylistic features*. A part of literary awareness resides in understanding what words mean as well as in understanding nuances of style.

As explained on page T18 of this book, each question and activity in the ODYSSEY program also has a label identifying the reading skill students will use when responding. These skills are **literal**, **interpretive**, and **critical thinking**.

Using Questions to Teach.
The question types described above are used in ODYSSEY mainly for teaching purposes, not testing. Most questions can start a series of responses, and one question may lead to another without interrupting the main topic of discussion. The resulting pattern of discussion may not be question–answer, question–answer, as it is likely to be in testing. Instead, the pattern for the discussion of a story may be the following: a question asking for clarification of a word or phrase leads to a question involving recall of the story events, which in turn leads to a question asking for an interpretation of a character's reaction to those events.

Try applying some of the following strategies during your classroom discussions:

1. *Probing.* A probe can be a request for additional information to clarify or elaborate on a response, or it can be a request for other answers. Such questions as ''Any other ideas?'' or ''Can you tell us *more* about that idea?'' can develop a discussion without fragmenting it. Listen to a response and decide whether a probe is needed.

2. *Requesting verification.* Ask students to return to the text in order to verify a point. Students may be asked to substantiate opinions as well as locate bases for statements of fact. At other times students may be called upon to use other sources, including their own experience, to verify a statement.

3. *Providing wait time.* The *wait time*, or *think time*, principle simply means that a time of silence comes between a question and a response.[2] Research shows that classes using wait time have better discussions. Responses are longer, and students show higher-level thinking than when the wait time principle is ignored.

To apply this strategy, you might begin by saying, ''Now I'm going to ask you a very thought-provoking question. Take time to think about it before you tell us what you think.'' Ask the question,

2. Linda B. Gambrell, ''Think-Time: Implications for Reading Instruction, *The Reading Teacher*, 34, no. 2 (November 1980); 143–146.

and then allow several seconds to elapse before calling for a response. *After* hearing a response, wait several seconds before commenting or asking for other responses.

EVALUATING READING EXPERIENCES

To evaluate whether your literature discussions, along with pre-reading preparation and silent, independent reading, are of benefit to the students, observe students on the following:

1. *Notice whether students seem to seek new reading experiences and whether literature lessons are eagerly anticipated.* If these reactions occur, the students are attaining the goals of the reading experience, which include pleasure, insight into human behavior, and appreciation for language.

2. *Consider students' responses during discussions.* Do they enter discussions enthusiastically? Do all contribute? Is there a give-and-take during the discussions that seems to produce a deepened understanding of the selection?

3. *Consider students' answers to the questions themselves, in order to identify their level of reading comprehension.* The literal level items (recall, vocabulary) are usually easy to evaluate since they call for *convergent* thinking. This means that students will come to an agreement on a "right answer." Though suggested "right answers" are provided in the Teacher's Edition, students' answers may vary and still be "right."

Above-literal items (inference, extrapolation, relating reading to experience) seek to develop *divergent* thinking. This means that students' answers will be different from one another since they are based on individual opinion and experience. Although examples of responses are presented in the Teacher's Edition and labeled "Possible answer(s)," no one should try to predict the range of good responses that can arise from divergent thinking. The following criteria can be used, however, in evaluating such responses:

- *Fluency.* Do students contribute easily to the discussion? Are they able to produce many responses?
- *Flexibility.* Are responses varied so that several *different* ideas are contributed?
- *Originality.* Are some students' responses creative as well as appropriate to the question; that is, do some students demonstrate unique ability to discern and to solve the problems posed by the question?
- *Elaboration.* When probed, can students expand their responses by adding details?

4. *Observe the students' responses to the reading through activities such as oral or written composition, dramatization, or creative expression in the arts.* If the reading experience and discussion are indeed promoting response to literature, activities will help reveal and develop such responses.

Additional Readings

Torrance, E. Paul, and Myers, R. E., *Creative Learning and Teaching.* New York: Dodd, Mead, 1970. Chapters 7 through 10 contain suggestions for asking good divergent-thinking questions, with factors to consider in evaluating responses.

Carin, Arthur A., and Sund, Robert B., *Developing Questioning Techniques: A Self-Concept Approach*. New York: Charles E. Merrill, 1971. The entire book contains helpful, practical suggestions for making discussion sessions popular and meaningful.

Sebesta, Sam Leaton, and Iverson, William J., *Literature for Thursday's Child*. Chicago: Science Research Associates, 1975. Part III contains a plan for integrating questions and activities of different types and levels.

Ruddell, Robert B., *Reading-Language Instruction: Innovative Practices*. Englewood Cliffs, N.J.: Prentice Hall, 1974. Chapter 11 includes transcripts and a guide to developing questioning strategies and promoting verbal interaction.

Written and Oral Composition

FROM RESPONSE TO COMPOSITION

Children and young people have much to say. They enjoy talking about what they have read. Their enthusiasm goes beyond the act of reading and answering a few questions about a literary selection.

Young readers may enjoy *retelling* a story, thus transforming the written form into oral language. They are likely to add a phrase here, change a word there, or *infer* a scrap of conversation or a detail of setting. Such alterations may not indicate a faulty memory at all, but rather show the teller's ability to reconstruct literature in imagination. Young readers may *extrapolate* from, or extend, a story. They may tell what might have happened after the story ended, or how it might have been different in another setting or situation. They may also relate the selection to their own experience, and thus *interpret* its meaning in terms of their own lives.

All of these types of responses have appeared in the oral and written responses of children and young people as they reacted to literature.[3,4] When such responses comprise a group of sentences with a central topic or purpose, they become a *composition*. A composition may be oral or written. It may be the product of an entire class, as when students dictate a paragraph to the teacher. It may be the product of a pair of students working together to stimulate each other's ideas and to share the speaking or writing task. A composition may also be done by an individual who either writes it down or dictates it into a tape recorder or to another person.

Preparing for Composition.   The preparation process for composition should begin orally, even if the result is to be a written product. An oral warm-up stimulates ideas through interaction. It permits immediate feedback and the chance to try out an idea before taking the effort and time to shape it completely.

At first, during the oral warm-up, students may use brainstorming techniques. Working in pairs or small groups, they are encouraged to say anything that comes to mind relevant to the assignment. Later in the warm-up, they review and evaluate what has been said.

It is good to remember, however, that some students work better alone during the warm-up time. These students need a period of quiet time to work uninterrupted on their ideas.

Where and When to Write.   The time and place for composition may vary according to your needs and those of your students. A writing corner, partially separated from the rest of the classroom, helps give some children inspiration and privacy for their task. Others are quite happy to remain with the group, perhaps gaining confidence through numbers. Some sit "properly" at their desks while others may capture the flow of ideas in a more informal, relaxed posture.

Some teachers like to assign a composition project, encourage warm-up for fluency, and then set the entire class to the oral or written composition task. While students work, the teacher circulates about the room offering individual help.

Other teachers make composition an ongoing process. Students may work on the assigned task at almost any time in the day. This

3. Alan C. Purves with Victoria Rippere, *Elements of Writing About a Literary Work: A Study of Response to Literature* (Urbana, Illinois: National Council of Teachers of English, 1968).

4. James R. Squire, *The Responses of Adolescents While Reading Four Short Stories* (Urbana, Illinois: National Council of Teachers of English, 1964).

plan has the advantage of permitting children to seize the moment of inspiration and work on an independent schedule. Its results are excitingly described in a classic book about creative composition, *They All Want To Write*, by Alvina Treut Burrows and three other teachers who experimented with the plan.[5]

THE ORAL COMPOSITION PROCESS

In the primary grades, oral composition is often spontaneous. For example, suppose a second-grade class had just read James Marshall's humorous story "Split Pea Soup," in which George is faced with eating his least favorite food every time he visits his friend Martha. The teacher may prepare the class for a composition assignment with a question such as, "What do you think Martha did the next time George came to visit her?" After inviting a number of answers, the teacher may suggest that the group compose a story about George's next visit. The group decides on one of the answers gathered from the discussion as story material.

Now the oral story process begins. If oral composition is a new experience, teacher and class may be satisfied with a few sentences describing the chosen incident. There is no "editing" and no rejection of ideas. It is more important to get each group member to contribute something to the story. As a follow-up, some children may perform the story as a puppet show (see page T43) while others illustrate the story.

Refining the Story.   Gradually these spontaneous story-making sessions can be modified and enriched. After the warm-up, two or three children can choose one of the story ideas and prepare to tell it before the group. Alternatively, the entire class can continue to work on a story, but this time the teacher might add some oral editing skillfully and unobtrusively.

Suppose, for example, that the group has just read "The Garden," one of Arnold Lobel's Frog and Toad stories (Level Two). Now the group is composing a story about what happens after Toad's seeds begin to grow in his garden. A main happening has been agreed upon: the seeds will grow into such large flowers that Toad's house will be covered. One child suggests as a first sentence for the story, "The flowers got so big that Toad couldn't find his house when he came home from the store."

Now the teacher can help extend and refine the story, "Why had Toad gone to the store in the first place?"

---

5. Alvina Treut Burrows, et al. *They All Want to Write: Written English in the Elementary Schools,* 3d ed. (New York: Holt, Rinehart & Winston, 1964).

Student 1: He went to buy a watering can.

Student 2: He bought some fast-grow pills he saw on television.

Student 3: A dog on TV said, "Give your flowers Quick Grow!"

Teacher: Now let's go back and start the story.

Student 1: Next day, Toad went to the store. He bought some pills to make his flowers grow. Then he bought a watering can.

Student 4: When he came back, he said, "Where's my house? All I can see is flowers!"

Student 3: A flower said, "Get out of here! I need that place where you are so I can grow."

Teacher: What did the flower look like—the one that said that?

Student 3: It was pink and it had a big tongue hanging out. . . .

As the story continues, the teacher can ask questions to help students organize and amplify it. There must be a give-and-take: encouragement to take risks, to try out ideas, and to alter the story when a "better" way is discovered.

THE WRITTEN COMPOSITION

If the story is deemed a success by its makers, the oral composition may merge into writing. In the primary grades, the teacher writes the story on the board or a note pad as students watch. Later the story can be copied onto a ditto master and duplicated. Each student can receive a copy to illustrate or to practice reading aloud.

Writing a First Draft.   The oral composition may also be transcribed by the students themselves. Many children move early toward independence in writing skills so that, after the initial warm-up, they can proceed on their own. Here, as in earlier stages, encourage risk taking and trial and error.

It is best *not* to ask that the first draft of a story, a poem, or a nonfiction composition be a finished product. Instead suggest that students begin writing by simply "filling a page" with attempts to start the composition in an interesting manner, with thoughts that need to be jotted down lest they be forgotten in the final writing, or with scraps of conversation or detail. Then, instruct students to prepare the first draft by writing on every other line, so that revisions can be made using the empty in-between lines.

Students should be free to scratch out and scribble in; they should be encouraged to attempt spelling words that they want to use, whether they can spell them correctly or not. Such use of "invented spellings" helps students achieve fluency and leaves them free to concentrate on expressing their ideas. Neatness and correctness are reserved for the final draft.

EDITING THE COMPOSITION

The trial and error of the composition process is a form of editing. When a first draft of a composition, oral or written, is planned and then reviewed for practice and improvement, editing is taking place.

Editing needs to be taught—and taught gradually. It is self-criticism, but criticism with a constructive purpose: to go over one's original creation with a listener's ear or a reader's eye to figure out how the creation can be improved. Editing is not correcting. It is reshaping, deciding whether a scene in a story ought to be changed in some way or whether a paragraph in a report belongs somewhere else. It is revising sentences and words that lack force or fail to say what is intended. For example, the teacher who asked the student to describe the flower in the discussion about Toad's garden was helping the child expand, and hence edit, his or her first oral draft. The child's original version, "A flower said, 'Get out of here!'" might therefore become "A big pink flower stuck its pink tongue out and said, 'Get out of here!'"

Developing Editing Skills at Intermediate and Upper Grades.
At intermediate grade levels and above, the skills of editing may be more directly taught. A series of questions like the following, organized by category, can be used according to what is to be stressed in a lesson.

Editing Story Structure.
- Does your story start at an exciting place?
- Would a certain scene be more interesting if you expanded it?
- Is there a scene that is too long?
- Would some of the story be lost if the scene were shortened?

Editing Conversation.
- Does the dialogue "sound" like spoken language?
- Is there conversation in your story that is just "filler" and could be left out?
- Is there a place where conversation needs to be added to increase suspense?

Editing Sentences.
- Is there a place in your story where you can help your composition flow by using one of these connector words or phrases: *so, therefore, if—then, because, since*?
- Can one sentence be combined into another to make the meaning clearer? (Note: Language arts textbooks provide sequences and practice in sentence *combining* and *expanding*. The emphasis in editing may be placed on the specific skills concurrently taught in the language arts text used in the class.)

Editing Words.
- Can you make your writing style more direct by striking out empty words such as *very* and *a lot*?
- Can you use a more specific descriptive term by finding a synonym in a thesaurus?

At upper grade levels, students may be introduced to proof-readers' marks such as those used for deletion, insertion, and new paragraph, along with the term *stet*, which means "do not make the change indicated." These aids to editing are in most dictionaries.

Correcting for a Final Draft.   To insist that everything spoken or written be perfect in mechanics can be stultifying, yet correct spelling, punctuation, capitalization, paragraphing, and all the rudiments of acceptable form must be taught.

The best way to teach mechanics without hampering fluency is to distinguish between *process* and *product*. During the composition process, emphasis should be placed upon creating—originating, exploring, and elaborating upon ideas. When the process yields a product that the child wants others to hear or read in finished form, the rules of correctness need to be followed.

Here are some helpful ways to teach mechanics:

1. *Have the students tape-record their speeches or hand in written first drafts of compositions*. You can listen to the recordings or correct the drafts, offering suggestions for improvement before the students present their work in final form.

2. *Encourage self-criticism*. Each student may be given an alphabetized list of words frequently used but sometimes misspelled. A recent source for such a list is Robert L. Hillerich's *A Writing Vocabulary of Elementary Children*.[6] A class dictionary is also a useful tool.

3. *Emphasize punctuation and handwriting when students prepare final copies of written compositions*.

Polishing the Oral Composition.   Oral compositions can be practiced with the aid of a partner who acts as director. The partner may suggest changes in delivery, identifying places where pace and force may be varied, correcting pronunciation, and offering an opinion about the general effect of the speech upon the audience.

One of the important values of the composition process is to enhance students' regard for literature through renewed interest in and enjoyment of stories and appreciation for an author's skill.

---

6. Robert L. Hillerich, *A Writing Vocabulary of Elementary Children* (Springfield, Illinois: Charles C. Thomas, 1978).

Additional Readings

Lewis, Claudia. *A Big Bite of the World: Children's Creative Writing*. Englewood Cliffs, N.J.: Prentice-Hall, 1979. Examples and theory of a composition program used in Bank Street College of Education and Portland State University, involving children from 3–12.

Tiedt, Sidney W., and Tiedt, Iris M. *Language Arts Activities for the Classroom*. Boston: Allyn & Bacon, 1978. Separate chapters give numerous examples and teaching ideas for writing, spelling, and listening, as well as ideas for using poetry and fiction.

Stewig, John Warren. *Read to Write: Using Children's Literature as a Springboard for Teaching Writing*. 2d ed. New York: Holt, Rinehart & Winston, 1980.

Smith, James A., and Park, Dorothy M. *Word Music and Word Magic: Children's Literature Methods*. Boston: Allyn & Bacon, 1977. A wealth of examples and techniques show integration of the best in modern and classical children's literature with the entire school curriculum, including composition.

Interpretive Reading and Dramatization

INTERPRETIVE ORAL READING

Sharing Interpretations. To interpret a story or poem well requires practice and concentration. The interpretive activity should follow careful silent reading of the selection and incorporate insights gained through discussion. Interpretive oral reading usually implies an audience—one or more listeners to whom the reader presents his or her interpretation.

The key to interpretive reading is *concentration*. Readers must learn to concentrate on finding the image and the feeling they want to impart and to work toward that goal. Here, then, are seven suggestions you can make to help students read interpretively:

1. *Find a selection, a stanza from a poem, or a scene from a story that you really want to read aloud to others.*

2. *Figure out why you have selected it.* If it is funny, what makes it funny? The language? The action? The surprise? If it is scary, what makes it so? Frightening words? A gradual build-up to a big scare?

3. *Now visualize the images or the pictures behind the words.* If you "see" the pictures in your mind as you read the selection aloud, your listeners will see them too. Sometimes it helps to tell yourself all about the pictures you imagine. Add ideas that the author did not tell you, using your imagination as you read.

4. *If the story or poem has action, try imitating the action as you practice reading.* Then leave out the movement and try to show the action with just your voice.

5. *Practice reading until you do not have to look at the words all the time.* Then read the selection to an empty chair three meters (approximately ten feet) or more away from you. Look often at the chair as you read. If the chair were alive, could it hear you? Would it like hearing the selection the way you are reading it?

6. For intermediate and upper grades: *Identify the purpose of each scene in a story or stanza in a poem.* Write one phrase that tells that purpose, for example, *to scare*, *to surprise*, or *to win sympathy*. Then, keep that purpose in mind as you read. Write the purpose on a sign and put the sign on your practice chair. Stop in the middle of your practice reading and ask yourself, "Am I reading to show that purpose?"

7. *After you have the pictures and the purpose in mind, try experimenting with the volume and pace of your voice.* Vary your voice from almost a whisper to almost a shout, from very fast to very slow. Then use some of this variety to help your listeners get the purpose in your reading.

Improving Oral Reading. Interpretive oral reading improves with praise if the praise is specific. "You read that with a great deal of expression" is not specific enough, it does not tell the reader what he or she did effectively. A more useful comment might be "I could hear the ghost rattling the dishes when you read that scene" or "I felt the sorrow of the man and woman when the girl told them she had to leave."

Interpretive oral reading also improves with good models. Most communities contain good models, so you may want to arrange readings by amateur or professional actors, senior citizens or parents with time and talent for reading aloud.

CHORAL SPEAKING

Drawing Upon the Flow and Feel of Words. "Star light, star bright, first star I've seen tonight. . . ." These simple, clear words, memory-cued by rhythm and rhyme, invite instant playback. The invitation "Now say it with me!" puts the choral-speaking mechanism in motion.

Almost every rhymed and metered poem in the primary grades can be enhanced through choral speaking. In addition, shared speaking encourages participation without risk. Shyness, fear of making mistakes, and the embarrassment of forgetting lines are all overcome as one speaks with the group.

This technique is also an aid to reading, particularly when used in the early years. As students recite together, they may rely partly on memory and partly on print to guide them. In this way, the "difficult" words become familiar in print.

Avoiding the Sing-Song Pitfall.   In choral reading, metered poetry may begin to sound "sing-song," a mere exercise in reciting rhythm without the intended interpretation of meaning. One way to avoid this pitfall is *not* to confine intermediate- and upper-grade choral reading to rhymed and metered poetry. An alternative is to let the sing-song pleasure of a metered poem run half its course, and then begin to introduce variety into the reading. Another is to concentrate on the poem's meaning. You might begin by reading a few lines of a poem and asking questions like these: "Who is saying these lines? How should the lines be said? In a puzzled voice? In a sad voice? With a laughing tone?" "What is happening in the poem? How can we show this feeling with our voices?" Such attention to meaning, even with nonsense poetry, will help direct the rhythm and sound away from sing-song and toward vocal variety in pace and volume.

Another way to avoid sing-song interpretations is to divide the choral reading so that *all* speakers do not read *all* of the lines. Some lines can be read in unison by all speakers, but some will be read by a sub-group or by one speaker.

PUPPETRY

Puppet shows hold fascination for children and adults. Students who a moment ago complained "I can't think of what to say" are suddenly released when "it is the puppets who do the talking."

Construction of Puppets.   In order to leave time for the production, select one of the following puppets, all of which can be made in a short time.

1. *Hand puppets*. A simple hand puppet may be no more than an old sock stretched over the hand and adjusted so that the curved palm of the hand opens and closes like a mouth. The face of the hand puppet can be dabbed on with tempera paint or constructed from yarn, buttons, and sewn-on shapes of cloth.

2. *Stick puppets.* A stick puppet may consist of a painted or cut-paper face on a flat surface such as a paper plate stapled or pasted on the end of a tongue depressor.

3. *Fist puppets.* A fist puppet is more elaborate than those mentioned above. The fist puppet's head is modeled out of papier-maché or other lightweight material, such as cotton or crushed paper with heavy paper covering. Features are applied with poster paint. The puppet's eyes should be larger than life to provide emphasis. A cardboard cylinder big enough to fit over the index finger is embedded at the neck of the puppet. The puppet's costume can be cloth cut and sewn to be gathered at the puppet's neck, with sleeves that fit over the puppeteer's thumb and fifth finger.

Practice and Performance.   Give students time to experiment with their newly constructed puppets—to play with voice and movement. When they are ready to perform, they may present the puppet show as Story Theater, where one or more readers read the story while puppeteers manipulate the puppets to show the action. The puppeteers may also perform the story on their own, using creative dramatics techniques to improvise dialogue and gesture. Finally, scripts may be selected or prepared: some students may read the speeches while other students manipulate the puppets; or the puppeteers may speak the puppets' dialogue as they manipulate them.

READERS THEATRE

In Readers Theatre—the term is usually spelled that way, without an apostrophe—students read orally from scripts that are often based on selections from literature. Play scripts, then, are especially suitable for reading with this technique, since characters' speeches are already indicated. The technique is also adaptable for use with stories and poems that contain considerable direct conversation.

Specialists in the Readers Theatre technique indicate that selections may be abridged or occasionally paraphrased for script purposes. They warn, however, that scripts are to be used only for specific performance; to circulate scripts extensively or to use them for wide public performance is against copyright law.

How It Works.   Similar to actors in a play, the performers in Readers Theatre "take roles"; they speak lines assigned to characters or to one or more narrators. But unlike actors, Readers Theatre performers do not move about a stage; they hold scripts in hand or place them on music stands or desks. A few gestures and changes in position are permitted if these help the interpretation, but the real effect of the literary selection must come from the readers' oral interpretation of characters and narration. Hence the suggestions for interpretive oral reading (page T41) are appropriate for Readers Theatre practice as well.

The Importance of the Director. The presentation can be improved by a good director who tells the readers how an audience might receive their efforts. Who should be the director? A student? The teacher? A parent volunteer? Any one of these will do if he or she can bravely but not threateningly stop the rehearsal at almost any point to offer advice: "I didn't *hear* how angry the two trolls were when Prince Lini refused them. Try that again" (*Half a Kingdom*, Level 4). Of course, the director must find a balance between expecting too much in a performance and permitting flaccid, unthinking reading. Students respond to direction that asks for, but does not demand, a lively, varied interpretation.

Finally, the finished production may be performed for an audience. Performers may sit or stand side by side, facing the audience, or they may position themselves so that two opposing characters face each other, the narrators off to one side and slightly closer to the audience. The audience, the performance area, and the likely arrangement of readers should be decided upon before final rehearsals begin, so that the readers feel they are working toward a well-planned, polished performance.

STORY THEATER

Interpretive oral reading is combined with "acting out" in Story Theater. One or more students read aloud the selection, which should be a story or poem with plenty of action. Simultaneously, a group of "players" performs the actions described in the reading. In addition, players may sometimes act as scenery. For example, several may portray a wall, a tree, or the window of a house.

How It Works. Story Theater begins with attentive reading and discussion of the story to be presented. Movement, or mime, can be encouraged as a natural extension of inference questions: "Show us how the lizard moves his head from side to side. Show how the hawk soars over the land, looking for the ring" ("The Wedding of the Hawk," Level 6). Roles are assigned or chosen by volunteers. Players develop their parts as they listen to the oral readers' rendition of the story; oral readers practice their skill until they can vary their pace to accommodate the pace of the players. The final performance, then, is a combination of oral reading and mimed action.

After its completion, the performance should be evaluated by the participants, using questions such as the following: *Which segments*

---

in the reading gave life to the story? What did the players do to make certain actions vivid? When a player was present but not specifically mentioned in a moment of action, what did he or she do? Did the player freeze, *standing still so that attention was directed to the action, or did the player* react *to what was happening? Would a different response have been more effective?*

The critique, or evaluation, may be followed by a second performance, and students may then note improvements.

Choosing Appropriate Selections.   For primary-grade children, Story Theater works well with nursery rhymes and other simple-action poems. It seems especially suited to folk tales that highlight action and do not contain a great deal of dialogue. Intermediate- and upper-level students, however, may wish to experiment with Story Theater productions in which players speak lines of dialogue.

CREATIVE DRAMATICS/IMPROVISATION

A story or a poem is read. During the discussion that follows, the teacher says, "*Show* us what you mean." A student gestures, mimes a series of actions, or speaks a line in a certain way to demonstrate a character or a description. From such a simple, brief beginning can come the activity often called *creative dramatics.* Creative dramatics is especially valuable for developing skills of inference, as students must infer the actions and motives that characters would be likely to display within the framework of the story.

First Steps.   Creative dramatics develops gradually. Begin by having students identify *one* crucial scene they would like to play. Then have them "try on" characters and develop gestures, facial expressions, and a manner of speech for each. Lines of dialogue may be quoted directly from the story, but memorizing should not get in the way of the playing. Instead, encourage players to *improvise* dialogue in the spirit of the story and scene.

Once the improvisation is under way, there may be a tendency for the scene to go on and on. If this happens, stop the action. (A signal from you, such as the single word "Curtain," can be used to stop the action without embarrassing anyone.) Immediately ask students to evaluate the playing: "What was strong in the playing? What seemed to be going wrong?" At this point, ask the group, players and observers alike, to reread the scene.

Insight into Character.   Geraldine Siks, an expert on creative dramatics procedure, offers a further suggestion: Have each player identify first the *big purpose* of his or her character in terms of the entire story, and then the character's *little purpose* in the scene that is being played. In addition, character traits and emotions should be discussed.[7] During this discussion, the focus should be on the characters, not the players. Say, for example: "The old man must show that he is terrified of the sea monster," not "You should act more terrified when you look at the sea monster."

Following evaluation, the scene should be replayed. Further evaluation should note, if possible, improvements in the playing.

The Need for Brief but Frequent Sessions. The single-scene sessions should be brief, perhaps no longer than ten minutes in primary grades and fifteen minutes in intermediate and upper grades. Frequent sessions, perhaps two per week, are recommended by most experts as the best way to move from the creative dramatics process to meaningful dramatic interpretation.

From Scene to Story. At all levels, dramatizing a single scene can lead to playing an entire story once the improvisation process runs smoothly. When an entire story is dramatized, pace and structure become more important than ever. The story must progress without having dialogue or action distract from its central focus. Winifred Ward, perhaps the best-known expert in the field of creative dramatics in schools, advises that planners and players must "concentrate on essentials," shortening or omitting scenes that contribute to the written story but do not move the drama forward. Scenes themselves often require "tightening," which involves highlighting the essential movement and dialogue while omitting the nonessential. Ward's basic evaluation question at this point is "Did the scene *move*?"[8] Attention must also be directed to the clear presentation of the story's problems in an early scene and to the build-up through successive scenes to a climax and solution.

Role Playing. An extension of creative dramatics is *role playing*, a technique that requires extrapolation. In role playing, a story is read up to the point at which a problem is encountered but not solved. Students discuss what the main characters will do about the situation. Roles are assigned, possible solutions are enacted, and the results are evaluated by asking, "Is this what the main characters *would* do? Is this what they *should* do?" When students return to the story, they do so with heightened interest, for they have taken an active part in predicting the story's outcome.

---

7. Geraldine Brain Siks, *Drama with Children* (New York: Harper & Row, 1977), p. 119.

8. Winifred Ward, *Playmaking with Children from Kindergarten Through Junior High School*, 2d ed. (New York: Appleton-Century-Crofts, 1957), p. 138.

PLAY PRODUCTION

The ODYSSEY literature program includes play scripts at every grade level. The play script is an increasingly popular literary form because it provides a direct avenue to participation in literature.

Informal Presentations.   In the classroom, a play script may be presented informally without scenery, costumes, or memorization, and with minimal movement. An informal presentation provides practice in characterization and timing. It also improves speaking skills, especially if readers must project their voices to an audience. The informal presentation can be enhanced if it is recorded on tape as a "radio play" with background music and sound effects. The tape may then be played for the readers' enjoyment and evaluation.

Formal Productions.   Formal production based on a play script requires much more time and planning, and it deserves an audience. It may also require a budget. Still, the excitement of a formal production of a play often makes the effort worthwhile. So, too, do the other rewards: the literary learning that results from extended close work with the play script, the confidence that arises from successfully portraying characters and incidents, and the poise that comes with performing in a company before an audience. (Students at the primary level need informal experience in drama before attempting a formal play production. Story Theater and creative dramatics should come first.)

Suggestions for a Successful Production.   Once a class has had some experience with formal play production on a small scale, the following suggestions may help guide more extensive productions.

1. *Make sure the class has had sufficient experience in oral interpretation and movement before they try to perform a play that requires extensive dialogue and a succession of scenes.*
2. *Make sure the class* likes *the play script.* Talk it over. Ask them to explain the dramatic appeal: "What might an audience like about this play?"
3. *Hold try-outs for all facets of the production, not just for acting roles.* Ask for volunteers to make scenery (drawn, painted, constructed, or hung as a backdrop), to be in charge of props, or to act as dialogue coaches. The actors themselves must be selected carefully, of course. Have them try out by improvisation rather than by reading lines. Ask pairs of students to assume the characters from the play and then to compose speeches and movements to fit a particular scene.

4. *With class participation, make a schedule for rehearsals*. The first session should consist of reading lines, with attention to oral interpretation of character. The second session should begin the *blocking* of action, determining characters' movements about the stage in each scene. In general, movement must be motivated, and a character should not move while another is speaking. "Stage business"—the use of props and gestures—is included in the blocking of action. At this point actors may carry scripts but they should also devote attention to memorizing lines. Subsequent sessions give practice, scene by scene, in dialogue and action.

5. *When planning scenery, costumes, and lighting, suggest rather than strive for actuality*. Setting may be suggested by scenery sketched on wrapping paper or merely by a backdrop consisting of a curtain or drape. An item of costume, such as a hat or an appropriate jacket, can suffice to designate a character. Lighting need not require footlights or spotlights, but the playing area should be clearly visible to an audience. The playing area itself can be a cleared area in the classroom if a raised stage is not available.

6. *Set aside time for a* dress rehearsal—*a session in which the entire production receives a run-through without interruption*. During this final rehearsal, the director may keep notes so that he or she can comment on the production afterward. The comments should be mainly positive, to encourage the players and crew to do their best. If the performance is to run smoothly, few changes should be made in the production at this point.

7. *Plan to present a formal production before an audience*. Besides offering a means for appreciating the considerable efforts of the cast, crew, and director, the production of a play is intended to provide entertainment for others. Some groups plan more than one performance, for increased experience before an audience.

A Word About Royalties.   Some plays, if presented formally, require payment of royalties. Be sure to check the title and copyright pages of a play script for a royalty statement before deciding to put the script into production.

A Sense of Accomplishment.   Allot time when the production is over for evaluating what was learned, what was especially satisfying, and what might be done "next time" to make the production process flow more smoothly. Teachers and other adults involved need to remember that play production in schools is for education, appreciation, and pleasure. A good question to consider is this: "Ten years from now will this play production be recalled by my students with pleasure and a sense of real accomplishment?"

Let it also be remembered that theater experience with literature is *direct* experience with literature. As author Tove Jansson has a wise character say in *Moomin's Summer Madness*, "A theatre is the most important sort of house in the world, because that's where people are shown what they could be if they wanted, and what they'd like to be if they dared to, and what they really are."[9]

Additional Readings

Coger, Lesley Irene, and White, Melvin R. *Readers Theatre Handbook: A Dramatic Approach to Literature.* Rev. ed. Glenview, Ill.: Scott, Foresman, 1973. Definitions, procedures, and "rules" for successful Readers Theatre productions, together with helpful case studies of how the procedures have succeeded in schools.

McCaslin, Nellie. *Creative Drama in the Classroom*, 3d ed. New York: Longman, 1980. This up-to-date edition gives reasons for using pantomime, improvisation, and creative dramatics.

Visual Arts, Music, and Literature

ART ACTIVITIES

The visual arts offer teachers and students a great variety of activities: drawing and painting, paper cutting, sculpting and modeling, constructing and printmaking. Any one of these can stir the students' imaginations and provide them with a visual means of responding to literature.

The teacher's choice of which art activity will enhance literary experience can be guided by class discussions of a particular selection. For example, if the discussion focuses on the *setting*, then students might sketch the setting or visualize it through collage. As they reread a description of a setting in a story or a poem, urge the students to develop a mental image. Then using pencil, crayon, pastel, charcoal, or other sketching instrument, they can sketch quickly on paper the scene in their imaginations. Following a discussion of a main character's traits, students might try to model that character from clay, not to show how the character looked but rather to reveal that character's individual qualities. A discussion of a poem's mood can lead to a painting or a collage.

9. Tove Jansson, *Moomin's Summer Madness* trans. Ernest Benn, Ltd. (New York: Avon Books, 1955), pp. 105–106.

MUSIC ACTIVITIES

The rhythms and sounds of words have their counterparts in the rhythms and sounds of music. Poems with strong rhythms or pleasant-sounding lines can inspire song making. To create songs from poems, have students read a poem several times to bring out the rhythm, phrasing, and mood. Use choral speaking techniques to do this. Then have students experiment with beat and sample melodies, progressing line-by-line through the poem. When the final song version is put together, tape the melody or quickly notate it above a written version of the poem.

Musical instruments can be used to create sounds that will heighten the mood for oral reading or any performance of literature. A ''signature tune,'' for instance, may announce the entrance of each character in the telling of a folk tale. Such tunes can be composed on a homemade xylophone, recorder, or kalimba. To stress the rhythm in a poem, use rhythm sticks, various types of drums, sand blocks, and maracas. Musical instruments may also be used to help establish the setting of a story or a play.

Listening to music may also enhance literary appreciation. To seek a literal tie between a literary selection and a musical selection is unnecessary. For example, no composer has written a symphony, ballet, or specific program music to accompany the Norwegian folk tale ''The Three Billy Goats Gruff'' (Level 1, Reader), yet children can find the troll and the setting of the drama in numerous works of the Norwegian composer Edvard Greig. Played before, during, and after the reading of a selection, such music adds impact while developing the students' listening abilities.

These are only a few of the boundless opportunities to promote literary appreciation and response through the visual arts and music. Boundless, too, is the pleasure to be gained.

Additional Readings

Gaitskell, Charles D., and Hurwitz, Al. *Children and Their Art*. 3d ed. New York: Harcourt Brace Jovanovich, 1975. This book presents a synthesis of child development and art development. It includes many examples that help explain how to encourage child development with art education.

Taylor, Gail Cohen. ''Music in Language Arts Instruction.'' *Language Arts* 58, no. 3 (March 1981): 363–367. This review of recent writing on the topic includes a section on music as an aid to story enjoyment and comprehension as well as a list of resources for teachers.

Poetry and the Teacher *Myra Cohn Livingston*

I am myself,
of all my atom parts I am the sum.
And out of my blood and my brain
I make my own interior weather,
my own sun and rain.
Imprint my mark upon the world,
whatever I shall become.

> Eve Merriam, "Thumbprint"

ROBERT FROST has written that a poem "begins in delight and ends in wisdom." The Irish poet James Stephens tells us that "What the heart knows today the head will understand tomorrow." In these words both poets suggest one of the most meaningful ways of introducing children to poetry: to infect with *delight,* stress the *joy,* approach through the *heart,* and know that wisdom and understanding will follow. It makes all the difference.

Children grow into poetry, beginning with Mother Goose. From the first time they hear rhyming verses that tell a small story, that play with words, that move along with bouncing rhythms, that stress rhyme, they are affirming a basic need to listen with both heart and movement—to respond with pleasure.

Jack be nimble,
Jack be quick,
Jack jump over
The candlestick.

Even nonsense poems allow them to test their own knowledge of what is true and what is not, to improve their self-images, and to be able to laugh both at others and at themselves:

Far and few, far and few,
Are the lands where the Jumblies live:
Their heads are green, and their hands
are blue;
And they went to sea in a sieve.

> Edward Lear, "The Jumblies"

New discoveries, thoughts, dreams, widely ranging emotions surround children as they grow up. Poetry mirrors their experiences through a more sophisticated handling of imagery, rhythm, and sound. What distinguishes poetry from other forms of literature is a rhythm that almost invites our bodies to move, our fingers to tap, our feet to dance; combinations of words that make us wish to repeat them aloud; rhymes, oftentimes, that encourage us to make up our own series of sounds; and a sort of irresistible music that engages heart, mind, and body. From the simplest folk rhyme to the ballad, from the traditional to the most experimental contemporary poem, poetry gives children room where their emotions and imaginations may run free.

DISCOVERING POETRY

The delight of poetry is in discovery: a new image, a different way of looking, the pleasure of words and rhythms used well, a humorous idea, an eccentric person, a striking metaphor. The delight is in the freedom to choose from among so many kinds of poems the ones that speak to us. The delight is in becoming familiar with riddles and limericks, haiku and counting rhymes, ballads and shape poems. The delight remains so long as children are able to come to a poem and find something of themselves and their world mirrored, extended, or even stretched. The delight allows them to act out the stories in pantomime or dance, to sculpt, to illustrate, to chant the words aloud, alone or with others, to try writing poems of their own, to respond in individual ways to the poetry they hear and read.

In the ten books of the ODYSSEY series, teachers will find verse and poetry to bring delight and pleasure. Here are traditional verses that have long been favorites of young readers, juxtaposed with verse by contemporary poets who write for today's young people. A mixture of light and serious verse spanning centuries and cultures has been selected within the thematic strands to afford a wide choice for both teacher and student. It may certainly happen that some of the selections will not appeal to every child or teacher. All of us hear a different tune. Some enjoy rhyming verse and ordered meter, while others prefer a freer, more open approach to poetry. Humorous verse, limericks, and riddles appeal to some; poetry with a more serious tone, a different mood, to others. Fortunately there are enough poems for all. Both teachers and students should always feel free to pick and choose what is meaningful to them as individuals.

It is here, I believe, that the wisdom and understanding of which Robert Frost and James Stephens spoke become important. Wisdom is *not* the message given by a poem to a reader; wisdom is *not* didacticism cajoling, exhorting, or instructing the reader of a poem to behave in a certain fashion; wisdom is *not* high-flown sentiments in lofty diction. Nor is wisdom

achieved by tearing apart a poem to find what figures of speech, what symbolism it may contain. Rather, wisdom is acquired by knowing that as we read poetry we grow in understanding. Wisdom is found by relating our thoughts and emotions as individuals to ourselves and to others about us, to other cultures, other centuries, other places. Wisdom comes in knowing that the best poetry has something to say for each of us if we first make the commitment to find the delight. Wisdom also implies that *com*prehending is not nearly so important as *ap*prehending. As John Ciardi has pointed out, it is important that we never ask "*What* does a poem mean?" but rather "*How* does a poem mean?" For Ciardi, the skillful combination of idea, form, words, and rhythm separates real poetry from mere pleasantries put into verse form.

Most likely we will not want to speak to children about methods of delighting or wisdom and understanding. What we can do is try to show them that poetry is part of life. Poetry has something to say about the way we view ourselves, our world, and everything in that world from a drop of rain to mirrors in the Fun House to our feelings about ourselves. Poetry can be funny, it can be sad. It is not, as many believe, a unit of study we get once a year filled with iambic pentameter and some poems to memorize.

Because of the increasing number of fine poetry anthologies available, it is possible for teachers in all grades to relate poetry to almost any subject. History might be studied using some of the folk poetry of America. Numerous poems deal with science and math. The ODYSSEY Teacher's Editions offer a wide variety of suggestions for integrating poetry with other arts—painting, dancing, creative writing, and dramatics, to name just a few.

Our most difficult job as teachers today may well lie in the need to elicit imaginative responses. In a world that promotes an unusual amount of passivity, reliance on mass media, and a great deal of programmed response, teachers need to touch the imagination of each child, to encourage this individual reaction to what is heard or read. In a single classroom there may be but a handful of children who respond to a given poem, but this reaction should be praised and nurtured. What happens when a poem and the right listener, the right reader, come together can be magic.

SHARING POETRY IN THE CLASSROOM

It will come as no surprise to teachers that few children today hear nursery rhymes at home. The classroom may well be the first place children hear poetry, and the teacher may well be the first person who reads poetry to them aloud. No matter what age or level of the students, poetry should be read aloud as often as possible.

Many of the poems in the ten ODYSSEY readers are suitable for individual and choral reading. Students can organize group readings of poems or memorize them for the joy of it. Many balk at the idea of memorization, but if a student especially likes a poem, the results can be wonderful! Whole classes have put on poetry programs to entertain other classes until the entire school becomes infected with the joy of performing. Again, if imagination is encouraged by the teacher, the students benefit not only from their personal response to poetry but grow with their hearts and minds to bring its enjoyment to others. Here are a few suggestions to help you get started.

1. *Choose poems you like and those you think your class will like.* Teachers cannot elicit enthusiasm for work they themselves do not enjoy. Be aware that riddles, limericks, and light verse will always be received well, but that other kinds of poetry will help young people grow in their perceptions and relationships with others.

2. *Encourage students to find verses and poems and share them with the class.*

3. *Experiment with different ways of reading the sounds and rhythms of poems.* One way to read a poem is to read each line as a separate idea followed by a pause.

Who has seen the wind? (pause)
Neither you nor I: (pause)
But when the trees bow down their
　　　heads (pause)
The wind is passing by.

> Christina Rossetti,
> ''Who Has Seen the Wind?''

Another way is to pause at the punctuation in a line. In this stanza, then, the question mark at the end of line 1 indicates a pause, as does the colon at the end of line 2. In the third line, however, one could either pause after the word *heads* or read the last two lines as one long sentence. There is no right or wrong.

4. *Don't be afraid to make mistakes when you read poems aloud.* Everyone does. If you flub a reading, pick up and start again—this will help minimize the students' embarrassment when they make mistakes in their own readings. Both teacher and students can learn together.

5. *Read with your heart rather than your head.* If you wish to laugh as you read, do so. When a poem is sad, don't hide your sadness; let it enter your voice just as you would let happiness.

Children know what emotions are—do not underestimate their ability to know if you are reading with honesty. They would much rather have a flawed, sincere reading from you than the perfectly enunciated recitation on a tape or record.

Don't be afraid to make the leap. Leave your head in arithmetic, in history, in social studies, in science; and bring your heart and sense of delight to poetry! You may astound yourself; you will astound your students—and together you will begin a love for poetry that you may never before have imagined possible.

Myra Cohn Livingston, ODYSSEY's poetry consultant, is Poet-in-Residence for the Beverly Hills Unified School District and a Senior Instructor at UCLA Extension. The author of thirty books, she has received many awards for her poetry, including the National Council of Teachers of English Award for Excellence in Poetry for Children, which was awarded her in 1980.

Bibliography

Books About Poetry

Ciardi, John. *How Does a Poem Mean?* Boston: Houghton Mifflin, 1959.

Hughes, Ted. *Poetry Is.* New York: Doubleday, 1970.

Kennedy, X. J. *An Introduction to Poetry.* 4th ed. Boston: Little, Brown, 1978.

Individual Poets

Bodecker, N. M. *Hurry, Hurry, Mary Dear! and Other Nonsense Poems.* New York: Atheneum, 1976.

Brooks, Gwendolyn. *Bronzeville Boys and Girls.* New York: Harper & Bros., 1956.

Clifton, Lucille. *Everett Anderson's Year.* New York: Holt, Rinehart & Winston, 1974.

Farber, Norma. *Small Wonders.* New York: Coward, McCann & Geoghegan, 1979.

Fisher, Aileen. *Out in the Dark and Daylight.* New York: Harper & Row, 1980.

Holman, Felice. *I Hear You Smiling and Other Poems.* New York: Charles Scribner's Sons, 1973.

Kuskin, Karla. *Dogs & Dragons, Trees & Dreams.* New York: Harper & Row, 1980.

McCord, David. *One at a Time.* Boston: Little, Brown, 1978.

Milne, A. A. *When We Were Very Young.* New York: E. P. Dutton, 1924.

Smith, William Jay. *Laughing Time: Nonsense Poems.* New York: Delacorte Press, 1980.

Thurman, Judith. *Flashlight and Other Poems.* New York: Atheneum, 1976.

Watson, Clyde. *Father Fox's Pennyrhymes.* New York: Thomas Y. Crowell, 1971.

Anthologies

Adoff, Arnold, ed. *My Black Me: A Beginning Book on Black Poetry.* New York: E. P. Dutton, 1974.

Behn, Harry, trans. *Cricket Songs.* New York: Harcourt Brace Jovanovich, 1964. Haiku attuned to young people.

Brewton, John E., and Blackburn, Lorraine A., comps. *They've Discovered a Head in the Box for the Bread and Other Laughable Limericks.* New York: Harper & Row, 1978.

Cole, William, ed. *The Birds and the Beasts Were There.* Cleveland: World, 1963. Poems about animals for every reader.

De la Mare, Walter, ed. *Come Hither.* New York: Alfred A. Knopf, 1957. A favorite collection of traditional poetry.

Houston, James, ed. *Songs of the Dream People: Chants and Images from the Indians and Eskimos of North America.* New York: Atheneum, 1972.

Wood, Ray, ed. *Fun in American Folk Rhymes.* Philadelphia: J. B. Lippincott, 1952.

Wordless Picture Books and the Teacher
Rosemary Salesi

Once upon a time there lived a little boy and a dog. They wanted to catch a frog for a friend and pet. They started down the hill and a branch was in there [their] way so the boy cut it down and put it in front of him. Then he started off again and right before him was a frog. He ran towards it and triped [tripped] over the branch and fell right into the water with dog and all. . . .

Sarah Shubert, First Grade

SARAH SHUBERT'S STORY, her own retelling of Mercer Mayer's book *A Boy, a Dog, and a Frog*[1] (in ODYSSEY Primer, Level 1), is just one example of how students can respond to a *wordless picture book*, a book in which pictures explain a concept or tell a story. Using invented spellings for some words, Sarah wrote her story after several short classroom activities: looking at the book; predicting what happened next in the story; and telling the story in sequence with the rest of the class. This lesson was in late March; for the previous three months, Sarah and her classmates kept diaries and wrote a short response paper each day. The few stories the first graders wrote, however, usually lacked a developed middle and an adequate ending; only a few were complete narratives. With the support of the plot, sequence, and characterization provided by Mercer Mayer's illustrations, well over half of the children wrote complete stories. Some, like Sarah, even observed the conventions of traditional storytelling, beginning with "Once upon a time" and ending with "And they lived happily ever after."

WHAT ARE WORDLESS PICTURE BOOKS?

For some teachers, the existence of wordless books and their use in the classroom may seem to be recent developments; but the first contemporary wordless picture books, such as Ruth Carroll's *What Whiskers Did*,[2] appeared in the early 1930s. In the 1960s and 1970s, many illustrators rediscovered this unique format and explored it further. They found that by using a series of sequenced illustrations with few or no words, they could introduce, develop, and eventually resolve a story problem. At this writing, over seventy-five illustrators have contributed wordless picture books to the growing body of children's literature, and each year brings more.

What is surprising about these books is their considerable variation in content, format, and style of art. There are two predominant types: *concept books*, which primarily deal with the alphabet, shapes, numbers, and such nonfiction subjects as

1. Mercer Mayer, *A Boy, a Dog, and a Frog* (New York: Dial Press, 1967).

2. Ruth Carroll, *What Whiskers Did* (New York: Henry Z. Walck, 1965).

the Apollo mission or a life cycle in nature; and *wordless stories*, which use sequenced pictures to move from an introduction of characters and problems to a climax and conclusion.[3] In a wordless story, the characters' facial expressions and actions aid the reader in deciphering the plot.

Teachers find wordless books to be an imaginative resource for promoting oral language development, storytelling, and writing skills at all grade levels. Students enjoy and think through the stories at the same time, and eventually most want to share the fun by retelling them to others.[4] Because the books call forth the children's own language, they provide opportunities for exploring concepts and creating stories.[5] The stories the children write can be used as reading material for the entire class. But perhaps most importantly, the use of wordless books can foster a positive attitude toward all books and reading.

Exposure to wordless books will benefit students now and in the future. In our visually oriented society, the ability to see the visual whole and the significance of each detail, as well as the ability to express oneself fluently, are needed by everyone.

THE TEACHER'S ROLE: GENERAL CONSIDERATIONS

Reading a wordless picture book should be an enjoyable experience for students. The student's language abilities and prior experiences, as well as the books themselves, will help determine success. In sharing these books, it is necessary to observe whether the children enjoy them. If the motivation of enjoyment is not there, avoid follow-up activities.

Except when used for lessons in making predictions, the entire book should be "read" initially without interruption. Since comprehension depends on how well the students perceive minor details and subtleties in a story, a second or third viewing, coupled with exploratory activities, will help students appreciate and respond to it more fully. Filmstrips of wordless picture books, such as those produced by Weston Woods Studios, Inc., enable large groups of students to enjoy the same story simultaneously and allow the teacher to focus attention on selected elements.

Beginning in the lower grades, wordless books can be used for step-by-step practice in describing characters and actions with words or phrases, then with one complete sentence, two or more sentences, and finally, with a number of sentences in logical order. Since many of the more sophisticated books can be read at either the literal or symbolic level, they work well in heterogeneous groups of students. For example, the problems that bilingual students have with books are lessened because they can label objects, describe actions, or write stories using their own languages. The books are so highly entertaining that the students may be more comfortable using their new language as they share ideas with each other.

3. Rosemary A. Salesi, "Reading, That's Easy. It's the Words That Are Tough," *Maine Reading Association Bulletin* (Spring 1973): 3–6.

4. Rosemary A. Salesi, "Books Without Words," *New England Reading Association Journal,* 9 (1973–74): 28–30.

5. Patricia J. Ciancolo, "Using Wordless Books to Teach Reading and Visual Literacy and to Study Literature," *Top of the News,* 29 (April 1973): 226–234.

SPECIFIC TEACHING SUGGESTIONS

The following are some ways to introduce students to wordless picture books. They may also help students gain independence for reading the books on their own.

1. *Suggest that students use the title to guess what might happen in the story.* This will help to prepare them for the events of the story.

2. *When using a wordless picture book that tells a story, be sure the students understand that the book does tell a story.* This is particularly important with preschool and early primary students.

3. *If the students are to work independently, encourage them to examine the entire book first, including the cover, endpapers, title page, and dedication page.* In some books, such as Peter Spier's *Noah's Ark*[6] and Diane De Groat's *Alligator's Toothache,*[7] the stories begin prior to the first page. Inferences are easier to draw when the student has examined the entire story.

4. *Encourage the students to look at illustrations closely and to note details.* Details in the illustrations foreshadow new events, changes in the action, or a subplot.

5. *Ask questions that students should ask themselves when they read alone:* What is happening? Why is it happening? What will happen next? Did I predict correctly? How do I know? What might the characters be saying to each other? What words would describe their actions and feelings?

6. *Have the students examine their wordless picture books several times and talk about them with classmates. Then ask them to close the books and tell the story.* If they use the book in storytelling, both children and adults tend to describe only the details in the pictures, completely ignoring the gaps that occur between them. Storytelling becomes more natural when the book is put aside because the storyteller is more apt to fill in the missing details and feel freer to improvise. The book's content thus provides a structure around which the storyteller can fashion his or her own stories. Creative responses should be praised.

Rosemary Salesi is a widely published author of professional articles and a reading workshop leader. She is currently an associate professor of education at the University of Maine at Orono, where she teaches courses in children's literature and elementary education. She was a classroom teacher for eight years.

Wordless Books for Primary Grades

Although the following selections are intended for primary grades, they need not be limited to a specific age or grade level. In most cases, students enjoy a wider range of wordless books as they mature. Children in preschool and early primary grades generally prefer realistic stories. Older, middle-school students enjoy these as well as the more sophisticated and fanciful books.

Anno, Mitsumasa. *Anno's Counting Book.* New York: Thomas Y. Crowell, 1977.

Briggs, Raymond. *The Snowman.* New York: Random House, 1978.

Carle, Eric. *Do You Want to Be My Friend?* New York: Thomas Y. Crowell, 1971.

Hoban, Tana. *Dig, Drill, Dump, Fill.* New York: Greenwillow Books, 1975.

Krahn, Fernando. *Sebastian and the Mushroom.* New York: Delacorte Press, 1976.

Sugita, Yutaka. *My Friend Little John and Me.* New York: McGraw-Hill, 1973.

Ueno, Noriko. *Elephant Buttons.* New York: Harper & Row, 1973.

---

6. Peter Spier, *Noah's Ark* (Garden City, N.Y.: Doubleday, 1977).

7. Diane De Groat, *Alligator's Toothache* (New York: Crown, 1977).

Resource Center

About the Authors and Illustrators

These notes present some information about the authors and illustrators in this book upon whom material was available. You may wish to read them aloud as you introduce the selections.

Merriam, Eve   For Eve Merriam, poetry is an exciting way to explore the everyday world. Her poems are about bugs and bears and dogs and wishes—all the things children enjoy. Eve Merriam has said: "When something is too beautiful or too terrible or even too funny for words: then it is time for poetry." In 1981 Eve Merriam won the National Council of Teachers of English Award for Excellence in Poetry for Children. She is well known for her books *Catch a Little Rhyme*, *It Doesn't Have to Rhyme*, and *There Is No Rhyme for Silver*.

Watson, Clyde   Clyde Watson became fond of Mother Goose rhymes and music while growing up in Vermont. Explaining her work, Clyde Watson says that she draws upon her childhood experience. "I love children and I write not specifically for children but to communicate in a certain way which children understand. Adults are beginning to understand the language of children's books, too." *Catch Me & Kiss Me & Say It Again* is one of her collections.

Welber, Robert   Robert Welber has owned an antique shop and produced plays in New York. He is also a teacher who decided to start his own school. At his one-room elementary school in New York, the Studio on Eleventh Street, children learn from each other and, with his help, teach themselves. Robert Welber's other stories are *Frog, Frog, Frog* and *Winter Picnic*.

Poetry for Reading Aloud

The following poems are recommended as related reading in the annotated lessons for this level.

COCKLES AND MUSSELS
A traditional Irish ballad

In Dublin's fair city,
Where the girls are so pretty,
    I first set my eyes on sweet Mollie
        Malone.
She wheeled her wheelbarrow
Through streets broad and narrow,
    Crying, "Cockles and mussels, alive,
        alive, oh!
        "Alive, alive, oh!
        Alive, alive, oh!"
    Crying, "Cockles and mussels, alive,
        alive, oh!"

She was a fishmonger,
But sure 'twas no wonder,
    For so were her father and mother
        before.

And they both wheeled their barrow
Through streets broad and narrow,
  Crying, ''Cockles and mussels, alive,
    alive, oh!
      ''Alive, alive, oh!
      Alive, alive, oh!''
  Crying, ''Cockles and mussels, alive,
    alive, oh!''

She died of a fever,
And none could relieve her,
  And that was the end of sweet Mollie
    Malone.
But her ghost wheels her barrow
Through streets broad and narrow,
  Crying, ''Cockles and mussels, alive,
    alive, oh!
      ''Alive, alive, oh!
      Alive, alive, oh!''
  Crying, ''Cockles and mussels, alive,
    alive, oh!''

WILL YOU BUY ANY TAPE?
A poem by William Shakespeare

  Will you buy any tape,
  Or lace for your cape,
My dainty duck, my dear-a?
  Any silk, any thread,
  Any toys for your head,
Of the new'st and fin'st, fin'st wear-a?
  Come to the pedler;
  Money's a meddler,
That doth utter all men's ware-a.

GREAT A, LITTLE A
An old rhyme

Great A, little a,
  Bouncing B!
The cat's in the cupboard,
  And can't see me.

HUMPTY DUMPTY
An old rhyme

Humpty Dumpty sat on a wall,
Humpty, Dumpty had a great fall.
  All the king's horses,
  And all the king's men,
Couldn't put Humpty together again.

JACK AND JILL
An old rhyme

Jack and Jill went up the hill,
  To fetch a pail of water;
Jack fell down, and broke his crown,
  And Jill came tumbling after.

LITTLE MISS MUFFET
An old rhyme

Little Miss Muffet
Sat on a tuffet,
Eating her curds and whey;
There came a big spider,
Who sat down beside her
And frightened Miss Muffet away.

A RIDDLE
A poem by Christina Rossetti

There is one that has a head without an eye,
  And there's one that has an eye without
      a head.
You may find the answer if you try;
  And when all is said,
Half the answer hangs upon a thread.

                    (A needle and a pin.)

Up and down,
Up and down,
Never touches the sky,
Never touches the ground.

> (A pump handle.)

What goes up the chimney down,
And can't go up the chimney up?

> (An umbrella.)

Which is correct:
> The yolk of an egg *is* white?
> The yolk of an egg *are* white?

> (Neither; the yolk of an egg is yellow.)

What's full in the daytime and empty at
night?

> (A pair of boots.)

THE FALLING STAR
A poem by Sara Teasdale

I saw a star slide down the sky,
Blinding the north as it went by,
Too burning and too quick to hold,
Too lovely to be bought or sold,
Good only to make wishes on
And then forever to be gone.

Professional Resources for the Teacher

Baskin, Barbara H., and Harris, Karen H. *Books for the Gifted Child.* New York: R. R. Bowker, 1980. An annotated list of almost 150 books for gifted children from kindergarten to upper grades, accompanied by several chapters on the historical and social problems of the gifted child.

Cianciolo, Patricia Jean, ed. *Picture Books for Children.* Chicago: American Library Association, 1973. This list of picture books is annotated with story synopses and art critiques. Categories of interest include Me and My Family, Other People, The World I Live In, and The Imaginative World.

Cullinan, Bernice E., et al. *Literature and the Child.* New York: Harcourt Brace Jovanovich, 1981. Along with selections of outstanding books, this book discusses criteria in choosing books for children and presents many practical teaching ideas.

Huck, Charlotte S. *Children's Literature in the Elementary School.* 3d rev. ed. New York: Holt, Rinehart & Winston, 1979. A reliable, comprehensive aid for understanding children's literature, for becoming familiar with classic and contemporary books, and for using books in the classroom.

Larrick, Nancy. *A Parent's Guide to Children's Reading.* 4th rev. ed. New York: Doubleday, 1975. An annotated listing of recommended books.

Livingston, Myra Cohn. *When You Are Alone/It Keeps You Capone: An Approach to Creative Writing with Children.* New York: Atheneum, 1973.

Lukens, Rebecca J. *A Critical Handbook of Children's Literature.* Glenview, Ill.: Scott, Foresman, 1976. Discusses the elements used to evaluate all literature—character, plot, setting, theme, point of view, style, and tone—and relates them to examples from children's books.

Moffett, James, and Wagner, Betty J. *Student Centered Language Arts and Reading, K–13: A Handbook for Teachers.* 2nd ed. Boston: Houghton Mifflin, 1976.

Recommended Reading for the Student

Most of the books recommended in this bibliography are available in hardcover. Some materials, however, are listed as paperbacks because they were originally published in that form or because a hardcover version was not available for review. All of the books are divided into the categories of **easy, average,** and **challenging,** which indicate the reading levels of these books. The category **read aloud** indicates books that a teacher might read to the students.

Easy

Anno, Mitsumasa. *Anno's Alphabet: An Adventure in Imagination.* New York: Thomas Y. Crowell, 1975. Letters of the alphabet, illustrated to look like wood, represent the beginning letters of unusual objects pictured on facing pages.

Carroll, Ruth. *Rolling Downhill.* New York: Henry Z. Walck, 1973. An easy wordless book about a dog and a cat playing with a ball of yarn.

Hoban, Tana. *Push Pull, Empty Full: A Book of Opposites.* New York: Macmillan, 1972.

Hutchins, Pat. *Rosie's Walk.* New York: Macmillan, 1968. Rosie the hen is pursued by a fox. A story of amusing visual sequences with few words. Filmstrip available.

———. *Changes, Changes.* New York: Macmillan, 1971. A wordless sequence showing wooden blocks transformed into a house, a boat, and a car. Filmstrip available.

Spier, Peter. *Fast-Slow, High-Low: A Book of Opposites.* New York: Doubleday, 1972.

Wezel, Peter. *The Good Bird.* New York: Harper & Row, 1966. Crayon-like drawings tell the story of the friendship between a bird and a goldfish. A wordless picture book.

Average

Ahlberg, Janet, and Ahlberg, Allan. *Each Peach Pear Plum.* New York: Viking Press, 1979. Hidden Mother Goose and folklore characters create a discovery game to enjoy with the rhymed text.

Carle, Eric. *The Very Hungry Caterpillar.* New York: William Collins & World, 1970. A caterpillar eats his way through the days of the week and the pages of the book until he changes into a butterfly.

Feelings, Muriel. *Jambo Means Hello: A Swahili Alphabet Book.* New York: Dial Press, 1974. African scenes are the backdrop for this alphabet book.

Fuchs, Erich. *Journey to the Moon.* New York: Delacorte Press, 1969. The first flight to the moon is pictured in beautiful paintings. A foreword gives the technical and historical information for the adult. A wordless picture book.

Galdone, Paul. *Henny Penny.* New York: Seabury Press, 1968. The familiar cumulative story is vividly presented.

Krauss, Ruth. *The Carrot Seed.* New York: Harper & Bros. 1945. No one except the youngest child believes his carrot seed will grow. A classic.

Marshall, James. *James Marshall's Mother Goose.* New York: Farrar, Straus & Giroux, 1979. Comical action and nonsense are combined in text and art.

Polushkin, Maria. *Mother, Mother, I Want Another.* New York: Crown, 1978. Though all a baby wants is another goodnight kiss, a mouse mother thinks he wants another mother, and she frantically tries to find her replacement.

Ungerer, Tomi. *Snail, Where Are You?* New York: Harper & Row, 1962. The spiral pattern of the snail appears in the illustrations, challenging the reader to look for that shape. A wordless book.

Challenging

Gág, Wanda. *The A B C Bunny.* New York: Coward-McCann, 1933. A bunny hops away from a storm and through the alphabet.

Lionni, Leo. *Little Blue and Little Yellow.* New York: Astor-Honor, 1959. A story of how two colors meet, mingle, and produce new colors.

Read Aloud

Alderson, Brian. *Cakes and Custard.* New York: William Morrow, 1975. A collection of well-illustrated Mother Goose rhymes.

Briggs, Raymond. *The Mother Goose Treasury.* New York: Coward, McCann & Geoghegan, 1966.

Deforest, Charlotte B. *The Prancing Pony: Nursery Rhymes from Japan Adapted into English Verse.* New York: John Weatherhill, 1968.

de Regniers, Beatrice Schenk. *May I Bring A Friend?* New York: Atheneum, 1964. Each time a boy joins the king and the queen for tea, he brings another funny animal friend.

Ginsburg, Mirra. *The Fox and the Hare.* New York: Crown, 1969. Who will help get the fox out of the hare's house? The only way is to outfox the fox.

Hoban, Russell. *A Birthday for Frances.* New York: Harper & Row, 1968. Frances deals with her jealousy as the family prepares to celebrate her sister's birthday. Another book about this lovable badger is *Bedtime for Frances.*

Lionni, Leo. *Frederick.* New York: Pantheon Books, 1967. Though Frederick dreams away the summer while the other field mice gather food, he stores up the sun's warmth and wonderful words that sustain the mice through winter.

McCloskey, Robert. *Make Way for Ducklings.* New York: Viking Press, 1941. The classic tale about two mallards finding a new home in the city for their ducklings.

McCord, David. *The Star in the Pail.* Boston: Little, Brown, 1975. Twenty-six poems about diverse topics—from starfish to snowflakes, from toads to fireflies.

Scott, Ann H. *On Mother's Lap.* New York: McGraw-Hill, 1972. Michael is troubled because a new baby brother is snuggling on his mother's lap.

Tresselt, Alvin. *Rain Drop Splash.* New York: Lothrop, Lee & Shepard, 1946. Raindrops gather into a puddle and flow from a lake to a river to the sea.

_____. *The Mitten.* New York: Lothrop, Lee & Shepard, 1964. A well-written version of the picture story that appears in this textbook.

Peppe, Rodney. *Three Little Pigs.* New York: Lothrop, Lee & Shepard, 1980. The familiar tale with humorous cartoon illustrations.

Related Media

The following key is used to identify the media listed below: **C**—cassette; **F**—film; **FS**—filmstrip; **R**—record. The catalog number immediately following each title should be used when ordering from the company identified in the entry.

Hutchins, Pat. *Rosie's Walk.* SF 125 (Weston, CT: Weston Woods Studios, 1972). **FS** with record or cassette.

_____. *Changes, Changes.* SF 154 (Weston, CT: Weston Woods Studios, 1973). **FS** with record or cassette.

Star Light,
Star Bright

Hello and
Good-bye

Where
the Clouds
Go

HBJ HARCOURT BRACE JOVANOVICH, PUBLISHERS
Orlando   New York   Chicago   Atlanta   Dallas

Star Light, Star Bright

ODYSSEY An HBJ Literature Program

The title of this book is from the traditional rhyme "Star Light, Star Bright" on page 63.

Sam Leaton Sebesta

Consultants

Elaine M. Aoki	Carolyn Horovitz
Willard E. Bill	Myra Cohn Livingston
Sonya Blackman	Daphne P. Muse
Sylvia Engdahl	Barre Toelken

Acknowledgments

For permission to reprint copyrighted material, grateful acknowledgment is made to the following sources:

Atheneum Publishers: "Wishing" from *There Is No Rhyme for Silver* by Eve Merriam. Copyright © 1962 by Eve Merriam.

Thomas Y. Crowell: "Knock, Knock" from *Father Fox's Pennyrhymes* by Clyde Watson. Text copyright © 1971 by Clyde Watson. "Riddle me, riddle me, what is that" from *The Golden Flute.*

William Heinemann Ltd. Publishers: "A,B,C, tumble down D" from *Cakes and Custard* edited by Brian Alderson.

Lothrop, Lee and Shepard Company: "Higher than a house," a Mother Goose rhyme, as reprinted from *The Arbuthnot Anthology of Children's Literature* by May Hill Arbuthnot.

Oxford University Press: "Rain on the green grass" from *The Oxford Dictionary of Nursery Rhymes* edited by Iona and Peter Opie (1951). "Sally go round the sun" and "Star light, star bright" from *The Oxford Nursery Rhyme Book* assembled by Iona and Peter Opie (1955).

Pantheon Books, a Division of Random House, Inc.: Condensed from *Goodbye, Hello* by Robert Welber. Copyright © 1974 by Robert Welber.

Random House, Inc.: "What kind of animals can jump higher than a house?" and "What goes up when the rain comes down?" from *Bennett Cerf's Book of Riddles* by Bennett Cerf. Copyright © 1960 by Bennett Cerf.

John Weatherhill, Inc.: "Why Rabbits Jump" from *The Prancing Pony* by Charlotte B. DeForest. Copyright 1967 by John Weatherhill, Inc.

Art Acknowledgments

Cover: Richard Brown.

4

Contents

Knock! Knock! Anybody There?

A rhyme by Clyde Watson

Knock! Knock! Anybody there?

I've feathers for your caps

And ribbons for your hair.

If you can't pay you can sing me a song,

But if you can't sing, I'll just run along.

Picture by Kinuko Craft

Happy Birthday to You

An old song

Happy birthday to you,

Introducing the Song *What is happening in the first picture?* (A girl is celebrating her sixth birthday.) *What is happening in the second picture?* (Some children may say that *another* girl is celebrating her sixth birthday, too.) *Now turn the page. What do you see?* (Twins are celebrating their birthdays.) *Let's sing ''Happy Birthday'' to Tina and Anna.*

Discussion Questions *How many times did you hear the words* Happy birthday to you? (Three.) *How is the twins' birthday like yours?* (Possible answers: they have a birthday cake; friends or relatives visit.) *Why do twins celebrate together?* (They were born on the same day.) *How is the twins' birthday different from yours?* (Possible answer: no twin to celebrate with.) *What do you like most about your birthday?*

Enriching Activity *Drawing.* Have the children draw three things they would like to do on their birthdays.

Pictures by Ted Rand

Happy birthday to you,

11

Happy birthday, Tina and Anna,

Point out the *piñata* /pēn·yät'·ə/ in the upper left corner of the facing page. Explain that it is a papier-mâché figure filled with toys and candies and hung in the air. The children, while blindfolded, take turns trying to break it to release its contents.

Happy birthday to you!

Rain on the Green Grass

An old rhyme

Objectives ● To note repetition in a rhyme. ● To relate a rhyme to personal experience.

Rain on the green grass,

And rain on the tree,

And rain on the housetop,

But not on me.

Introducing the Rhyme *Do you know any rhymes to say when it rains?* ("Rain, Rain, Go Away.") *A long time ago, people thought rhymes would charm away the rain. Here is another old rhyme that's been said on rainy days for many years.*
Discussion Questions *How many times did you hear the word* rain? (Three.) *Where do you go when it rains?* (Possible answers: inside; under an umbrella.)
Enriching Activity *Drawing.* Have the children draw what they like to do when it rains.

What Goes Up?

A riddle

Objectives ● To enjoy a riddle. ● To recognize opposites used in a riddle.

What goes up

when the rain comes down?

(An umbrella.)

Picture by Tony Kenyon

15

Sally Go Round the Sun

An old rhyme

Objectives ● To recognize repetition of words and actions in a rhyme. ● To interpret a rhyme with movement.

Sally go round the sun,

Sally go round the moon,

Sally go round the chimney-pots

On a Saturday afternoon.

Introducing the Rhyme *Here is an old rhyme that children used in a circle game. Listen to the rhythm of the words. Feel how the words help you move around in a circle.*
Word to Know
  chimney-pot: (See the annotation on the facing page.)
Discussion Questions *What words are repeated?* ("Sally go round.") *What did Sally go around?* (The sun; the moon; the chimney-pots.)
Enriching Activities **1.** *Movement.* Have the children clasp hands, walk in a circle, and chant the rhyme. At the end of the rhyme, they reverse the movement. One child as "Sally" moves around outside the circle in the opposite direction. Another circle game is "Ring Around the Rosie." **2.** *Oral extension.* Have the children discuss how this rhyme could be used in a game. For example: After "Sally" goes around the circle, the children might scatter; the child "Sally" tags becomes the next "Sally." **3.** *Extending experiences.* Have the children tell what they might do on a Saturday afternoon.

Picture by Jane Teiko Oka

16

Point out the chimney-pots on the chimneys in the illustration. Explain that they are made of clay or metal. When placed on top of a chimney, a chimney-pot increases draft and reduces smoke.

17

Jack Be Nimble

A Mother Goose rhyme

Objectives ● To enjoy a Mother Goose rhyme. ● To interpret a rhyme with pantomime.

Jack be nimble,
Jack be quick,
Jack jump over
The <u>candlestick</u>.

Introducing the Rhyme *What Mother Goose rhymes do you know?* (Possible answers: "Jack and Jill"; "Simple Simon"; "Little Bo-Peep.") *Mother Goose rhymes are very old, and some have words that may not be familiar to you. This rhyme is called "Jack Be Nimble."* Nimble *means "able to move quickly." Let's read the rhyme to find out why Jack must be nimble.*

Word to Know
   candlestick: a holder for a candle.

Discussion Question *Why must Jack be nimble?* (To get over the candlestick.)

Enriching Activities **1.** *Pantomime.* Have one child jump over a candlestick or other object as the class recites the rhyme, replacing "Jack" with the child's name. **2.** *Echo poem.* Divide the children into two groups. Have one group recite a line and the second group repeat it. Complete the rhyme in this way. Have the children repeat the rhyme the same way, but quickly this time. **3.** *Related reading.* See pages T62 and T63 for titles of Mother Goose books.

Jumping over a candlestick was a way of telling fortunes. If you jumped over the candlestick without knocking it down, you would have good luck for a year.

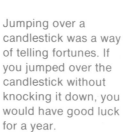

18

Picture by Jane Teiko Oka

19

Tell a Story
At Home

Objectives ● To identify what might have happened and to predict what may happen next to characters in an illustration. ● To infer information from an illustration. ● To act out situations suggested by an illustration.

Background This illustration is designed to stimulate classroom discussion. This lesson is one way to guide the discussion.

Discussing the Picture *We are going to make up our own story for this page by telling what is happening in the picture. When does the story take place?* (At eight o'clock in the morning.) *Where does the story take place?* (Possible answers: in a house; in an apartment.) *Who is in the picture?* (A father, a mother, and a little girl.) *What is this family doing?* (Encourage discussion of details.) *What may the family do next?* (Possible answers: Father will go to work; Mother will go to work; the girl will go to school.) *What do you think the family was doing before this picture?* (Possible answers: the family woke up; got dressed; had breakfast; fed the pets.) *How is this picture like your house on a school morning? How is it different?*

Enriching Activities **1.** *Pantomime.* Ask the children to pantomime morning activities or things they do on a rainy or snowy morning. Have the class guess what is being acted out. **2.** *Drawing/sequencing.* Have the children divide large pieces of paper into three sections and draw scenes of before, during, and after breakfast.

Picture by June Goldsborough

21

Objectives ● To enjoy a story in verse.
● To identify sequence in a story. ● To
relate a story to personal experience. ● To
recognize a story pattern.

Synopsis of the Story A child observes
young animals leaving their mothers to learn
about the rest of the world. The child follows
the same pattern by going to school.

From Good-bye, Hello

A story in verse by Robert Welber

Reading Level Challenging

Pictures by June Goldsborough

A kitten goes creeping
Away from the rug.

Good-bye, Mother.
Hello, bug.

23

A mouse goes out
To climb and see.

Good-bye, Mother.
Hello, tree.

A bird begins
To try to fly.

Good-bye, Mother.
Hello, sky.

A squirrel comes running
Down the tree.

Have the children look at the picture and fill in the words *Hello, bee.*

Good-bye, Mother.
Hello, bee.

29

A child is watching
Each little creature.

Good-bye, Mother.
Hello, teacher.

Questions

What did each one see?

Discussion Questions *The kitten, the mouse, the bird, and the squirrel all did some things that were the same. What were those things?* (Left their mothers; said ''Good-bye, Mother''; made new friends.) *What did the girl in the pictures do after watching the animals?* (Left her mother; said good-bye; went to school.) *Whom, besides the teacher, might the girl meet at school?* (Possible answers: friends; new classmates; the principal.)

1. I saw the   tree   bee   bug

2. I saw the   teacher   tree   sky

3. I saw the   bug   sky   bee

Enriching Activities **1.** *Rhyming.* Help the children make up rhymes that tell about times they left home, such as to play in the snow or to visit grandparents, and what new things they found. Have them follow the "Good-bye, _____ / Hello, _____" pattern.

2. *Drawing or painting.* Have the children draw or paint other young animals leaving their mothers and finding new things. Help the children add short rhymes to their drawings following the "Good-bye, Hello" pattern.

4.   I saw the   bee   teacher   tree

5.   I saw the   bug   sky   teacher

Questions 1–5 focus on **Literal / recall** skills. **1.** Bug. (page 23)
2. Tree. (page 25)
3. Sky. (page 27)
4. Bee. (page 29)
5. Teacher. (page 31)

Activity   **Critical / relating to experience**   *Drawing or painting.*

Draw or paint a picture to show something *you* saw today.

33

Tell a Story
At School

Objectives ● To infer information from an illustration. ● To recognize reading opportunities in different environments.

Background This illustration is designed to stimulate discussion about reading and literature in the classroom. This lesson is one way to guide the discussion.

Discussing the Picture *What is happening in this classroom? (Encourage discussion of details.) What did the children in this picture have to know before they could give a puppet show? (Possible answers: the story; how to make puppets and a puppet stage.) What books do you see in the picture? (The Three Bears; The Three Pigs; Humpty Dumpty; Billy Goats Gruff; The Gingerbread Man.)*

Picture by Ted Carr

34

Enriching Activities **1.** *Reporting.* To help the children recognize that books are only one reading source, have them recall where they saw words to read that day.
2. *Puppetry.* Read aloud Leo Lionni's *Frederick* (Pantheon, 1967) and help the children plan a puppet show for the story. See the puppetry section on page T43.

A, B, C, Tumble Down D

A Mother Goose rhyme

Objectives • To identify the speaker of a rhyme. • To make up an ending for a rhyme.

Introducing the Rhyme *I want you to guess who is saying this rhyme. As I read the rhyme, look at the picture.*

A, B, C,
Tumble down D,

36

Word to Know

cupboard (kub′·ərd): a closet or cabinet with shelves for dishes or food.

Discussion Questions *Who do you think is saying the rhyme?* (The mouse.) *How do you think the mouse feels?* (Safe; happy.) *Why?* (Because the cat can't see it.)

Enriching Activities **1.** *Rhyming.* Begin another alphabet rhyme and ask the children to help finish it. For example: "H, I, J, tumble down K,/The (*bird's*) in the cupboard and can't (*fly away*)." **2.** *Related reading.* See pages T62 and T63 for titles of alphabet books.

The cat's in the cupboard
And can't see me.

As early as the fifteenth century, many rhymes were designed to help children learn their ABC's. This rhyme was used by young and old when playing "battledore and shuttlecock" (an early form of badminton played with a paddle). See page T60 for another version of this rhyme.

Picture by Sharon Harker

37

A B C Mystery

Objectives ● To identify alphabet letters.
● To match letters and letter sounds with literary characters.

Introducing the Lesson *There is a big mystery in Storyland. Nine letters are missing! Let's go through the alphabet in the picture and pick out the missing letters. Look at the picture. Try to find who took each letter and where each one can be found.* (A—Raggedy Ann, in her pocket; B—the Three Bears, on a chair at their table; F—the fox, in his mouth; G—Goldilocks, on her apron; H—Humpty Dumpty, on his belt; J—Jack and Jill, in the water splashing out of their pail; M—Miss Muffet, near her skirt; R—Red Riding Hood, in her basket; W—the wolf, in his paw.)

Enriching Activities **1.** *Making books.* Have the class make an *A B C Book of Story Friends.* **2.** *Oral extension.* Ask for volunteers to tell what they know about the characters in the picture. See page T60 for the rhymes "Humpty Dumpty," "Jack and Jill," and "Little Miss Muffet."

Nine letters are missing!

Raggedy Ann™ took the **A.**

Who took the other letters?

NOPQRSTUVWXYZ

Tell a Story
It's Halloween!

Objectives ● To infer information from an illustration. ● To interpret a theme by imagining oneself in a similar situation.

Background This illustration is designed to stimulate classroom discussion. This lesson is one way to guide the discussion.

Discussing the Picture *Are you ready for some fun? We are going to tell what's happening on this page. What time of the year is it?* (Autumn.) *What holiday is being celebrated?* (Halloween.) *What is happening in the picture?* (Possible answers: a sack race; bobbing for apples; dancing; one ghost scaring another.) *Who are the people in the picture?* (Possible answers: children in costumes; witches; ghosts; pumpkin heads.) *What else do you see in the picture?* (Encourage discussion of details.) *How can you tell that the characters are having a good time?* (Possible answers: they are smiling; laughing; dancing.) *How would you feel if you were there?*

Enriching Activities 1. *Drawing/oral extension.* Have the children draw any characters or creatures they would like to be on Halloween. Then have them imagine being those characters and tell what they will do.
2. *Pantomime.* Have each child make a simple paper mask or prop and act out the part of a character in the picture. Have the class guess what each child is portraying.

40

Picture by Kinuko Craft

41

Five Little Pumpkins

A rhyme

Objectives • To identify different characters' points of view. • To identify mood in a rhyme. • To interpret a rhyme through choral speaking.

Introducing the Rhyme *This is a Halloween rhyme. How can you tell that just from looking at the picture?* (Pumpkins and jack-o'-lanterns are in the picture.) *What time of day is it?* (Early evening.) *What are the pumpkins doing?* (Sitting on a fence; smiling.) *Turn the page now. What is happening in the sky?* (It's getting darker; witches and bats are flying through the sky. Encourage discussion of the picture's details.) *Turn the page. What has happened now?* (Possible answers: the wind is blowing; the lantern light is out; the pumpkins are rolling away.) *Let's turn back to the first picture of the pumpkins. I'll read the rhyme to you so we can find out why the pumpkins rolled away.*

Pictures by Christa Kieffer

Five little pumpkins
Sitting on a gate,
The first one said,
"Oh, my, it's getting late."

The second one said,
"There are witches in the air."
The third one said,
"But we don't care."

The fourth one said,
"Let's run and run and run."
The fifth one said,
"I'm ready for some fun."

"Oo-oo!" went the wind
And out went the light,
And the five little pumpkins
Rolled out of sight.

Discussion Questions *Which pumpkins seemed to be a bit frightened in the rhyme? What did they say?* (The first: "Oh, my, it's getting late"; the second: "There are witches in the air"; the fourth: "Let's run and run and run.") *Which pumpkins seemed ready for fun?* (The third: "But we don't care"; the fifth: "I'm ready for some fun.") *What things in the pictures make the scenes look scary?* (Possible answers: witches, bats, a scarecrow, a dark house, the sky.)

Enriching Activities **1.** *Extending experiences.* Have volunteers tell about times when something, such as weather or other schedules, interrupted their play. **2.** *Choral speaking.* As the class recites the narration in the rhyme, have five children hold paper jack-o'-lanterns up to their faces and say the pumpkins' lines. **3.** *Puppetry.* Help the children make pumpkin finger puppets from construction paper.

47

Riddle Me, Riddle Me

Two riddles

Objectives ● To identify opposite words as clues to a riddle. ● To demonstrate the meanings of opposites with movement. ● To make up riddles.

Introducing the Riddles *There are two riddles on these pages. The first riddle is on the left-hand page. Look closely at the picture and listen for two words in this riddle that mean the opposite of each other. Try to*

Riddle me, riddle me, what is that,
Over the head, and under the hat?

(Hair.)

guess the answer to the riddle from the picture and the words. Read the first riddle; then ask the first two **Discussion Questions.** *Now let's try the next riddle. It's a tricky one, so listen carefully.*

Discussion Questions *What words are opposites in the first riddle?* (Over and under.) *What is the answer to the first riddle?* (Hair.) *What is the answer to the second riddle?* (All kinds of animals—houses cannot jump.)

Enriching Activities 1. *Movement.* Have the children use movement to demonstrate the meanings of such opposites as above/below, up/down, and in/out; for example, they might sit *on top* of a table, then go *underneath* a table. **2.** *Making riddles.* Read aloud the riddles on pages T60 and T61, having the children find the clues and guess the answers. Then have the children make up riddles. Help them choose word opposites, common objects, or experiences to use in their riddles. **3.** *Related reading.* Share with the children the book *Fast—Slow, High—Low: A Book of Opposites* by Peter Spier (Doubleday, 1972). **4.** *Making books.* Have the children add the riddles they have written and the riddles in their textbook to their riddle books.

What kinds of animals can jump higher than a house?

Pictures by Stan Tusan

All kinds of animals.
Houses cannot jump.

49

Why Rabbits Jump

An old Japanese rhyme

Objectives • To identify a question and an answer in a rhyme. • To respond to a poem by following a question-answer pattern.

"Why are you rabbits jumping so?
　　Now please tell why, tell why."
"We jump to see the big round moon
　　Up in the sky, the sky."

Background According to Japanese legend, the great mother of rabbits comes from the sky and plays in the sea once a year. If she visits on the eighth day of the eighth month and under a full moon, many rabbits will be born the next year.

Picture by Ed Taber

Introducing the Rhyme *What is happening in this picture?* (Rabbits are jumping.) *What is smiling in the sky?* (The moon.) *"Why Rabbits Jump" is an old Japanese rhyme. Some Japanese believed the rabbit had something to do with the moon. Let's ask these rabbits why they are jumping.*

Discussion Questions *What question did we ask the rabbits?* ("Why are you rabbits jumping so?") *What was the rabbits' answer?* ("We jump to see the big round moon up in the sky.") *What other animals can jump?* (Possible answers: kangaroos; fleas; frogs.)

Enriching Activities **1.** *Choral speaking.* Separate the class into two groups. Have the first group of children recite the first two lines of the rhyme. Then have the second group say the last two lines. Reverse the groups for a second recitation. **2.** *Oral extension.* Ask the children to think of questions they would ask animals and have volunteers make up possible answers.

The Mitten

A Ukrainian folk tale retold in pictures by Willi Baum

Introducing the Story *Name some animals you know and tell me what kind of house they live in. (Possible answers: bees, a hive; bears, caves; dogs, doghouses.) Many animals have homes. But the animals in the story* The Mitten *find an unusual home.* The Mitten *is a folk tale that has been told for a long time in the Ukraine, a part of Russia. You can read this story by looking at the pictures.*

After the children read the story silently, you may want to have them tell it aloud in their own words, as suggested in the first **Enriching Activity** on page 60. Begin the story as follows, calling on a child to continue: *Once upon a time on a cold winter's day in Russia, a boy named _____ put on his warm coat, hat, and mittens and went to the forest to gather wood. . . .*

53

54

57

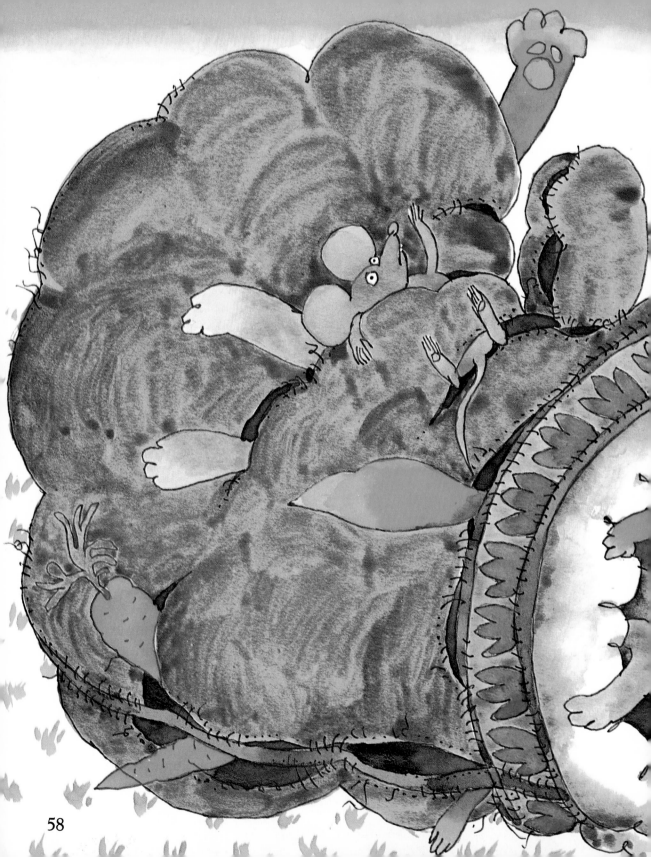

59

Discussion Questions Have the children fill in the words in parentheses. *A young boy drops* (a mitten). *It is found by* (a mouse). *The mouse is joined by* (a squirrel). *The squirrel points out that* (a rabbit) *is coming. The rabbit is followed by* (a fox and its cub). *The mitten looks full, but a tiny* (bug) *wants to come in. The mitten bursts. It is found by* (the boy). *What was the surprise at the end of the story?* (The mitten burst.) *Why did the mitten burst?* (Possible answer: because too many animals were in the mitten.) *Look at the last picture in the story. What do you think will happen next?* (Possible answer: the mouse will use the hat as its new home.)

Enriching Activities **1.** *Flannelboard story.* Using simple flannelboard figures, have three children retell the story. Ask one child to tell the beginning; another, the middle; and the third, the end. Help them add dialogue and name the characters.

2. *Storytelling.* Have the class compose a cumulative story patterned after *The Mitten.* Use a picture or object, such as a toy robot or car, to help them begin.

60

Objective ● To recognize that a riddle may have more than one answer.
Introducing the Riddle *Children have tried to figure out the answer to this riddle for many years. Can you figure it out?*

Higher Than a House

An old riddle

Discussion Question *What do you think the answer is?* (Tell the children to look at the picture for answers.)
Enriching Activities **1.** *Oral extension.* Have the children think of what they might see in the sky that children of long ago did not see. Answers may include satellites or rockets. **2.** *Making books.* Have the children add the riddle in their textbook to their riddle books.

Higher than a house,

Higher than a tree,

Oh, whatever can that be?

(Many answers,
such as a star,
the moon, a spaceship.)

People long ago found in the moon, the stars, and the clouds signs of what was to come. Rhymes were made up about some of them.

Picture by Jane Teiko Oka

Star Light, Star Bright

An old rhyme

Objectives ● To recognize the subject of a poem. ● To recognize an unusual turn of words that creates a surprise. ● To relate poems to personal experience.

● To compare poems about similar subjects.
Introducing the Rhyme *Have you ever watched the stars at night? Sometimes you can see many stars. People often wish on the first star they see. Sometimes they say this rhyme.*
Discussion Questions *When would you say this rhyme?* (When you had a wish to make.) *What wish would you make if you wished on a star?*
Enriching Activities (See page 64.)

Star light, star bright,

First star I see tonight,

I wish I may, I wish I might,

Have the wish I wish tonight.

63

Wishing

A poem by Eve Merriam

If I could have

Any wish that could be

I'd wish that a dog

Could have me.

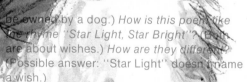

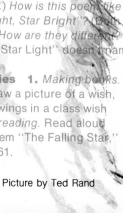

Picture by Ted Rand